Cambridge Elements ≡

Elements in Publishing and Book Culture
edited by
Samantha Rayner
University College London
Leah Tether
University of Bristol

ABORIGINAL WRITERS AND POPULAR FICTION

The Literature of Anita Heiss

Fiannuala Morgan
Australian National University, Canberra

CAMBRIDGE
UNIVERSITY PRESS

University Printing House, Cambridge CB2 8BS, United Kingdom

One Liberty Plaza, 20th Floor, New York, NY 10006, USA

477 Williamstown Road, Port Melbourne, VIC 3207, Australia

314–321, 3rd Floor, Plot 3, Splendor Forum, Jasola District Centre,
New Delhi – 110025, India

79 Anson Road, #06–04/06, Singapore 079906

Cambridge University Press is part of the University of Cambridge.

It furthers the University's mission by disseminating knowledge in the pursuit of
education, learning, and research at the highest international levels of excellence.

www.cambridge.org
Information on this title: www.cambridge.org/9781108747691
DOI: 10.1017/9781108779579

First published 2021

A catalogue record for this publication is available from the British Library.

ISBN 978-1-108-74769-1 Paperback
ISSN 2514-8524 (online)
ISSN 2514-8516 (print)

Aboriginal Writers and Popular Fiction

The Literature of Anita Heiss

Elements in Publishing and Book Culture

DOI: 10.1017/9781108779579

First published online: January 2021

Fiannuala Morgan

Australian National University, Canberra

Author for correspondence: Fiannuala Morgan, Fiannuala.Morgan@anu.edu.au

ABSTRACT: Wiradjuri woman, Anita Heiss, is arguably one of the first Aboriginal Australian authors of popular fiction. A focus on the political characterizes her chick lit; and her identity as an author is both supplemented and complemented by her roles as an academic, activist and public intellectual. Heiss has discussed genre as a means of targeting audiences that may be less engaged with Indigenous affairs, and positions her novels as educative but not didactic. Her readership is constituted by committed readers of romance and chick lit as well as politically engaged readers who are attracted to Heiss's dual authorial persona; and, both groups bring radically distinct expectations to bear on these texts. Through analysis of online reviews and surveys conducted with users of the book-reviewing website Goodreads, I complicate the understanding of genre as a cogent interpretative frame, and deploy this discussion to explore the social significance of Heiss's literature.

KEYWORDS: publishing studies, genre, chick lit, Aboriginality

ISBNs: 9781108747691 (PB), 9781108779579 (OC)

ISSNs: 2514-8524 (online), 2514-8516 (print)

Contents

1 Introduction

In 2007, Australia's Racial Discrimination Act was suspended in the Northern Territory to allow for the implementation of the Intervention: policy that included deployment of military personnel to Aboriginal towns and communities, withholding of welfare payments, prohibitions of customary law in bail, and sentencing and bans on pornography and alcohol, amongst others (Scott and Heiss, 2015).[1] This was an extraordinary measure. The establishment of the Act in 1975 had sought to partly redress and protect ethnic and cultural groups from the discrimination previously enshrined in Australian policy. It was more than a statement of good intentions, and for Aboriginal and Torres Strait Islander peoples, subjected to greater legal discrimination than any other minority group in Australian history, it contributed directly to the advancement of Indigenous rights with the eventual establishment of native title in the Mabo case of 1992.[2] Despite the advances and language of the reconciliation movement, the Intervention represented both the re-emergence and the endurance of racist Australian policy.

It was against this context that Wiradjuri academic and poet, Anita Heiss, published the first of her four-part chick lit series: *Not Meeting Mr Right*. The purple cover of the 2007 publication features an image of a woman with flaming red hair, dressed in a little black dress, sitting

---

[1] Dependent on context, this manuscript uses the language Aboriginal and Indigenous. Indigenous refers to both Aboriginal Australians and Torres Strait Islander people.

[2] Lieutenant James Cook declared Australia as property of the British Empire at Possession Island in the Torres Strait in 1700. This claim to ownership was based on the legal fiction of *Terra nullius* (land belonging to no one), which declared that the land was uninhabited and, thus, viable for occupation. Two hundred years later Eddie Koiki Mabo challenged this legal ruling, thereby affirming in the eyes of the law that Australia was always Aboriginal country. The transformative potential of the ruling was later significantly restricted by amendments that identified numerous grounds for the extinguishment of the native title. Despite this, the Mabo ruling remains significant as a partial acknowledgement of some of the injustices of the past.

coyly as abstract representations of men fall from a conveyor belt below her red stilettos. Similar imagery was to adorn the covers of the subsequent three novels: *Avoiding Mr Right* (2008), *Manhattan Dreaming* (2010) and *Paris Dreaming* (2011). For each, these paratextual elements, including their promotional blurbs, belie the novels' political intensity.

Academic and industry understandings of the genre present the pursuit of a career, love and shopping as uniformly constitutive of chick lit. That is, through first-person narration, an urban-based woman heavily invested in consumer culture 'comes of age' or 'consciousness' through episodes of dating (Yardley, 2006: 4). Each of Heiss's texts certainly adheres to this generic description, featuring a different Aboriginal female protagonist in pursuit of love, career and general fun. In *Not Meeting Mr Right*, Alice Aigner – Head of History at a Sydney Catholic girls' school – undertakes an exhaustive search for Mr Right, determined to be wed by her thirtieth birthday. In *Avoiding Mr Right*, Peta Tully – Department Manager of Media, Sports, Arts, Refugees and Indigenous Affairs – relocates from Sydney to Melbourne to pursue her career aspiration of one day becoming Minister of Cultural Affairs. Along the way she escapes a stifling relationship and finds love with an unconventional character – a policeman! In *Manhattan Dreaming*, Lauren – an up-and-coming curator at the National Aboriginal Gallery of Canberra – undertakes a fellowship at the National Museum of American Indians in New York City in flight from an unhealthy relationship with a Canberra-based footballer. And, in *Paris Dreaming*, Lauren's colleague Libby, the programme manager at the National Aboriginal Gallery, undertakes a fellowship at Musée du Quai Branly in Paris. Although declared to be on a 'man fast' (2) and a 'realist' not a 'romantic' (12), Libby ultimately finds love with Jake Ross, First Secretary to the Australian Ambassador.

As much as these novels are about dating, shopping, career and international travel they also feature fiercely and unapologetically political themes and content. In *Not Meeting Mr Right* this entails constructions of Aboriginality and a complication of Australian history. In *Avoiding Mr Right* there is a focus on Aboriginal deaths in custody and the institutionalization and exploitation of Aboriginality as a field within academia. *Manhattan Dreaming* and *Paris Dreaming* both foreground the role of art by Aboriginal artists in maintaining and celebrating culture as well as deconstructing reductive and stereotypical understandings of Aboriginality. In the same year that both images and accounts of Aboriginal community dysfunction dominated the mediascape, courtesy of the Intervention, Heiss was presenting an alternative – a representation of Aboriginality that was successful, urban, career-driven and middle-class. The juxtaposition of event and publication is not necessarily causal, but it is significant. Despite sixteen years of formal commitment to reconciliation, settler Australian conceptions of Aboriginality remained dominated by deficit discourse,[3] 'a mode of thinking ... that frames Aboriginal identity in a narrative of negativity, deficiency and disempowerment' (Fforde et al., 2013: 162).

For the purposes of this book, the significance of Heiss's novels lies not singularly in the presentation of a counter stereotypical representation of Aboriginality, but also in the strategy, intent, presentation and marketing of these texts in the genre of chick lit. Heiss is arguably the first Aboriginal Australian author of popular fiction. This classification has implications not only for the internal logics of the novels but also for their readership. As argued by Ken Gelder in his seminal study *Popular Fiction: The Logics and Practices of a Literary Field* (2004), 'a writer produces popular fiction because he or she intends (or, would prefer) to reach a large number of readers' (22). For decades, Aboriginal authors have been writing narratives that defy stereotypical representations of Aboriginality. Although her protagonists are fictional, Heiss draws on a tradition of Aboriginal female

---

[3] The process of reconciliation in Australia formally began with the establishment of the Council for Aboriginal Reconciliation in 1991. Guided by the vision of 'a united Australia which respects this land of ours; values the Aboriginal and Torres Strait Islander heritage; and provides justice and equity for all,' the Council established a ten-year time frame to advance the national process of reconciliation. Very basically, reconciliation is an ongoing process that encourages the 'coming together' of Australians based on mutual understanding, recognition and respect. In 2001 Reconciliation Australia, an independent not-for-profit organization, was established to continue the council's work. Their vision for reconciliation is based on five inter-related dimensions: race relations; equality and equity; unity; institutional integrity; and historical acceptance ('Reconciliation Action Plan').

authors who write in the confessional mode. In her memoir, *Am I Black Enough For You?*, Heiss reflects on this writing process, noting that 'my expression of identity is translated onto the page as the story unfolds' (2012: 219). What is significant about Heiss, however, is that she is strategically electing to write into the genre of chick lit, thereby taking an overtly political message – a message that defies dominant deficit understandings of Aboriginality – to a mainstream audience.

Previously, Heiss had published in diverse formats such as children's literature (*Who Am I? The Diary of Mary Talence*, 2001), poetry (*Token Koori*, 1998) and satire, exemplified in the collection *Sacred Cows* (1996). Her PhD dissertation, later published by Aboriginal Studies Press as *Dhuuluu-Yala: To Talk Straight-Publishing Indigenous Literature* (2003) is an exploration of the Australian publishing industry as it relates to Indigenous authors. In this landmark study she clearly identifies systemic difficulties facing Indigenous authors publishing fiction works focused on Indigenous issues, ideas and themes, in particular the mistaken notion that there is a circumscribed readership for Indigenous authored texts. In her memoir (2012), she describes her desire and decision to write chick lit novels as strategic and measured:

> my strategy in choosing to write commercial women's fiction is to reach audiences that weren't previously engaging with Aboriginal Australia in any format, either personally, professionally or subconsciously. And it is that non-Indigenous female market that is key to my audience. Let's face it, there are not enough Blackfellas to sustain any publishing venture, least of all an entire genre. With this in mind I made a conscious decision to move into the area of commercial women's fiction, releasing four books in the genre of chick lit. (215)

Reinforcing her strategic approach to genre, Heiss's own authorial persona adds another important dimension to the significance and reach of these novels. She inhabits a multitude of positions in the Australian literary field, thereby appealing to a broad and differentiated audience. Heiss has moved between the academic and literary fields at different points in her career and has resisted or remained largely ambivalent about qualification of a singular professional category.

Her personal website, Anitaheiss.com, describes her as 'an author, poet, satirist and social commentator', and as a 'creative disruptor' (2018). In an article published in the *Sun Herald* in 2008, Catherine Keenan wrote of her conversation with Heiss, 'the only question that really seems to stump her is when I ask what her job is. Usually, she says she's a writer, which is true, but doesn't quite cover it.' Indeed, Heiss is also an academic – now Professor of Communications at the University of Queensland – and an activist, a public intellectual and an Ambassador for Indigenous Literacy, amongst other roles. In her memoir Heiss demurs, 'I don't even consider myself an academic, even though I've jumped through all the hoops' (2012: 109), but her academic institutional affiliations and PhD in literature bolster her authority as a public advocate and intellectual on Indigenous affairs. Ultimately, she is an individual who is able to leverage the discursive power of one space – and translate this into another. Her chick lit novels can be interpreted as both an extension and departure from her academic material and imply a diverse readership; including those who are committed genre readers and those who are drawn to her work as an academic and public intellectual. Primarily, this breadth of appeal and focus constitutes the focus of this book: it is about chick lit, representations of Aboriginality and the Australian reader. In particular, it is about genre as strategic practice for an author who inhabits a multitude of authorial positions in the Australian literary field and as an interpretative frame for her diverse and differentiated readership.

1.1 A Tradition Challenged: Non-White Chick Lit

This book aligns with the theoretical aims of Erin Hurt's excellent edited collection *Theorising Ethnicity and Nationality in the Chick Lit Genre* (2018a). Hurt notes that 'while scholars have addressed the attraction chick lit held, and holds, for readers, this genre remained undertheorized in key ways, especially with regard to ethnicity and nationality' (2018a: 7). Hurt's collection is a careful interrogation of what constitutes 'cultural citizenship' in chick lit novels from across the globe; Australia, Saudi Arabia, America and East and Southern Asia. It is an exciting intervention into a previously whitewashed genealogy of the genre that begins with Helen Fielding's *Bridget Jones's Diary* (1996). Cumulatively it demonstrates how a white-centric framework *can* lead to productive, but often incomplete, readings of non-white articulations of the genre: 'whiteness implicitly becomes the norm when chick lit scholarship treats ethnicity and race as a focus rather than a framework, thus implying that race and ethnicity are secondary or optional elements when analysing chick lit' (10).

In opposition to Yardley's more generalized definition of the genre, Hurt extends the scholarship of Pamela Butler and Jigna Desai (2008) to identify a transnational unity in these narratives that is defined by the ascendency of neo-liberalism. In effect, they are neo-liberal fairy tales. As argued in her article, 'Cultural Citizenship and Agency in the Genre of Chica Lit and Sofia Quintero's Feminist Intervention' (2017): '[these novels] represent individual action as capable of solving systemic problems . . . that do not accommodate inequality on a social and cultural level' (15). This claim, in Hurt's opinion, extends to other forms of ethnic chick lit (2018a: 6). Ultimately, her appraisal of the genre is not entirely pessimistic: 'the goal here is not to discredit or dismiss the genre as a purveyor of these fantasies – since these fantasies are generated by neoliberalism as a protection mechanism to hide real systems of oppression – but rather to understand why protagonists and readers desire these fantasies and continue to feel attached to them' (7). By decentring a theoretical focus on post-feminism for neo-liberal feminisms, transnationalism and intersectionalism, many of the essays in the collection affirm the novels' significance through attention to their internal politics.

This Element represents both an extension and a departure from Hurt's approach. My analysis attends more closely to the reader, as well as the author's own understanding and navigation of genre. Ultimately, this is a localized study that is grounded in the politics of the Australian context and does not seamlessly map onto transnational readings of chick lit. Indeed it is my contention that while scholars must remain mindful of industry definitions, terms such as ethnic chick lit (and subgenre classifications: chica lit, sistah lit, etc.) only reify these narratives as deviations or subversions of their white – and implicitly normative – counterparts. This Element proposes a distinct approach to chick lit, genre and popular fiction. I argue that straight ideological or textual analysis, that is, a reading of the politics of Heiss's novels, would be insufficient to adequately capture and underscore the significance of these works. In opposition to this approach, I propose a sociological model of literary analysis that holistically accommodates the nexus of gender, race, author, text and reader. Heike Mißler employs a comparable approach in *The Cultural Politics of Chick Lit: Postfeminism and Representation* (2016), especially in her attempt to privilege the voice of readers of chick lit. Through analysis of chick lit blogs and online fan communities, Mißler asks 'how they make sense of their genre' (3). Her study is an ambitious and global survey of the political significance of the genre. My own study is more localized: both geographically and in focussing attention on genre as strategic practice.

Methodologically, this approach is loosely inspired by Bourdieu's sociology of literature (1993, 1996) and supplemented by critical scholarship on genre, critical race theory, Australian Indigenous studies, postcolonial literary theory, reading studies and an extended interview with the author. In his three-tiered analysis of *A Sentimental Education* Bourdieu undertakes a reading of the internal logics of the novel, a consideration of the literary field, and finally, an analysis of the author's habitus. For my own analysis of Heiss's literature I re-interpret this approach to focus on three key areas aligned with my own definitions: the author; the page; and the reader. I follow Bourdieu's line in asserting that an ideological reading of the text, or any kind of purely internal interpretation, does not suffice. I agree, too, with his suggestion that 'it can only be an unjustifiable abstraction to seek the source of the understanding of cultural productions in these productions themselves, taken in isolation and divorced from the conditions of their production and utilization' (Bourdieu, 1988: xvii). Therefore, any analysis of a literary text must take into account factors in its production and reception. As expressed by Johnson (1993) in his summary of the *Field of Cultural Production*, 'to be fully understood, literary works must be reinserted in the system of social relations which sustains them. This does not imply a rejection of aesthetic or formal properties, but rather an analysis based on their position in relation to the universe of possibilities of which they are a part' (11). In so doing, I avoid essentialist understandings of the text and push against a universal or ahistorical conception of literature. My Element, thus, engages with the complex network of social relations that make the existence of the text possible (Johnson, 1993: 10).

In accordance with Heiss's desire to 'reach audiences that weren't previously engaging with Aboriginal Australia in any format' (2012: 215), I pursue the questions: What power does Heiss's chick lit bear for producing personal transformation in the reader? Just who is reading her novels, and to what effect? I am interested in how this question plays out with reference to available discourses and understandings of Aboriginality, Australian history, racial identity and belonging within the Australian context. I conduct thematic discursive analysis of book reviews collected from Goodreads.com and further inform this analysis with surveys then conducted with Goodreads reviewers to move beyond an abstract consideration of these questions.

Heiss positions her literature, both academic and popular, as a pedagogical tool. In an interview conducted with the author she explains, 'I want [settler audiences] to learn things, but I want all my books to teach in some way' (2017). However, her approach is more evocative of the language of reconciliation, with an emphasis on understanding, assistance and discussion, than it is bluntly didactic: 'I'm trying to create something that has a lasting life and will be used in classrooms to generate conversations and help people understand their role in society' (Heiss, 2017). Although I am interested in the idea of the education of the reader (Mathew, 2016b), I supplement this with a focus on the concept of the cultural interface, first developed by Martin Nakata but integrated into Australian literary studies by Anne Brewster (2015) as a productive site of cross-racial and cultural negotiation (Nakata, 2007). Through my analysis of Goodreads reviews of Heiss's novels I adapt this approach for online communities and extend contemporary scholarship in reading studies that considers book clubs as democratic sites of discussion. This Element, then, presents a sustained complication of academic understandings of chick lit, genre and of popular fiction. Drawing on the work of Hans Robert Jauss and Elizabeth Benziger (1970) and John Frow (2006), I propose an understanding of genre as a regulative frame. Genre, as a 'fuzzy' and 'historically contingent' organizational practice (Frow, 2006: 80), is something imputed by the reader to the text that operates to contextualize and delimit its interpretation. While I do not seek to advance a new definition of genre in this Element, I do put forward an understanding of genre as a framing device as inspired by Frow's analysis.

This is not to suggest, however, that different genres do not possess constitutive thematic and rhetorical elements. There are a number of different academic and industry definitions of chick lit. In this Element, I take up Ann Steiner's (2008) definition of the genre: 'good chick lit novels are defined as fun, witty, easy and light reads dealing with real issues. Readers have to be able to sympathise with the main character; identification is, of course, the foundation of the genre' (par. 33). Steiner's definition of the genre is sufficiently porous to facilitate a reading of Heiss's literature that can account for both the author and reader's subjective experience.

1.2 Aboriginal Popular Fiction

In the year directly following the publication of Heiss's first chick lit novel, Australia's cultural and political landscape shifted markedly. Eleven years of conservative liberal rule ended with the ascendency of a Labor government. Newly appointed Prime Minister Kevin Rudd's leadership began optimistically with a declaration that the government's first orders of business would include the acknowledgement of truth contained in the *Bringing Them Home Report* (1997) and the delivery of a formal apology to members of the Stolen Generations.[4] The report, commissioned under the leadership of Labor Prime Minister Paul Keating (1991–6), but inherited by a Coalition administration, exposed the reality of the forced removal of Indigenous children from their families throughout the twentieth century. On 13 February 2008 Rudd issued a formal apology to the Stolen Generations. He not only offered his condolences for the actions of past governments, but also expedited an intervention in national storytelling and narratives (Butler, 2013: 3). Rudd's apology represented a turning point in public history and issued a direct challenge to those Australians who had denied the truth of Indigenous testimony.

---

[4] The Stolen Generations are the Indigenous children who were forcibly removed from their families by the Australian government. This assimilationist policy endured throughout the twentieth century.

For some, this acknowledgement marked the loosening of the stagnated debate of the Australian History Wars: public debate driven by academics, public intellectuals and the mainstream press that contested the extent to which colonization had impacted, and continued to impact on Australia's Indigenous peoples. What eventuated was a seeming moment of cultural cognitive dissonance, a space opened up for greater reception of Indigenous testimony and narratives. At the same time, mainstream media representations and policy articulation of Indigenous deficiency continued to proliferate and circulate. The *Closing the Gap* policy (implemented April 2007), successor to the Reconciliation movement, now can be read retroactively as further compounding deficit understandings of Aboriginality (Fforde et al., 2013: 166).

Heiss's novels reflect the tensions and dissonance inherent in this moment. In *Paris Dreaming* (2011), for example, protagonist Libby outlines the significance of the Apology for the increased status of Aboriginal art: 'it was as if Rudd had endorsed a greater interest in Aboriginal art and culture' (49), but the novel also highlights the Apology's role in fostering a level of unintentional political apathy among settler Australians. Reflecting on poor attendance at the Sorry Day Memorial Walk, Libby's mother surmises, 'I reckon since the Apology, the pressure's off people to march so much, like it's all over now and they don't have to remember' (97).

Since concluding her four-part chick lit series Heiss has gone on to produce other popular fiction novels. These include *Tiddas* (2014) and the historical romance *Barbed Wire and Cherry Blossoms* (2016). The earlier chick lit novels, however, were arguably significant in demonstrating the viability of mainstream Aboriginal literature and other cultural forms. Heiss's novels navigate the incommensurability of the pervasive political situation: a growing desire for narratives of Aboriginal resilience and survivance are confounded by media portrayals and government policies that continue to reinforce deficiency. In the years following the publication of her chick lit novels there has been a surge in numbers of Aboriginal authors writing, publishing and producing in fields of popular fiction and other mainstream cultural forms: Ambelin Kyawmullina's *The Tribe Series* (Young Adult 2012–15); Claire Coleman's *Terra Nullius* (Science Fiction/ Speculative Fiction 2017); Nicole Watson's *The Boundary* (Crime 2011); as well as the Australian Broadcasting Commission (ABC) television series *Redfern Now* (2012–15) and *Cleverman* (2016–17). Analysis of Heiss's chick lit provides the opportunity to explore a moment of origin in developing mainstream interest in Aboriginal popular fiction.

This Element is composed of three sections that cumulatively account for the nexus of the author, text and reader. In the second section I consider the author within the Bourdieusian concepts of position taking and strategy in order to unpack the differentiated authorial positions that Heiss inhabits within the Australian literary field. To add to how agents assume different positions within the literary field, Bourdieu develops the idea of strategy as distinct from rules. As articulated by Anderson (2016: 695), 'in his theory of practice Bourdieu accounted for the differences he identified between what people did and what the rules suggest they would do by using the term *strategy*'. Bourdieu is primarily concerned with how cultural products contribute to the reproduction of the social order; however, as argued by Hockx and Smits (2003), Bongie (2008), Brouillette (2016) and Dalleo (2016) his delineation of the literary field as governed by either the principle of economic gain or literary prestige does not allow for the possibilities of opposition and critique. I draw on the work of Huggan (2001), Boschetti (2006), Dalleo (2016) and Casanova (2004) to broaden the parameters of the literary field to incorporate this political dimension. Instead of presenting a broad re-conceptualization of the Australian literary field, I draw on Heiss's dissertation *Dhuuluu-Yala: To Talk Straight* (2003), and my own conversations with the author, to present an understanding that 'what is at stake' in Heiss's literature is not just market success, but also the power that literature yields for social transformation. That is, the engagement of her readership in complex representations of race and history in the Australian context. This section attends to the distinctiveness of the position that Heiss inhabits in the Australian literary field inclusive of diverse mechanisms of artistic legitimation: the university, the publishing industry; and reviews of her chick lit published in newspapers and literary journals. First, I draw on Lahire's (2010) conception of the 'second job' (450) to explore how Heiss's academic career has supplemented and continues to inform her authorial identity and practice. Second, I explore her understanding of genre as strategic practice and, finally, I consider critical reviews of Heiss's literature that demonstrate a dissonant understanding of her authorial persona. These reviews reflect an interpretative divide delineated between an affirmation of the political dimension of her work and criticism of its articulation as popular fiction.

Scholarship on chick lit emphasizes the genre's political significance as a way of redressing the hierarchy of literary value implicit in the academy. In the third section I suggest that a purely ideological and genre-based approach is restrictive in that it reduces enquiry to either the question of adherence or deviation from formula, or to simplistic enquiry into the feminist credentials of the text. This approach proves particularly problematic when applied to non-white articulations of chick lit that are invariably discussed as distinct, deviant or subversive. Through a reading of the limited scholarship written on Heiss (Ommundsen, 2011; Mathew, 2016; O'Mahony, 2018), alongside the work of Anne Brewster (2007, 2008, 2015) and Martin Nakata (2007) and consideration of the literary field outlined in Section 1, I propose an approach that replaces an internal reading of the novels with a focus on the reader herself. I take up Frow's articulation of genre as a 'frame', that operates to guide reader expectations. This approach allows for a consideration of the social significance of the novels, rather than just their internal politics.

Beginning with Janice Radway's *Reading the Romance: Women Patriarchy and Popular Culture* (1984), this final section draws on recent theorizations of the reader to explore the social significance of Heiss's chick lit. I am interested in how the reader engages with the literature of Anita Heiss with respect to the discussion undertaken in the sections on The Author and The Page that concerns representations of race. In particular, I am interested in how readers attend to the political dimension of her novels. As raised over the course of this Element, a focus on reader response is a productive movement away from the limitations of genre scholarship. In this section I analyse reader reviews collected from the book reviewing website Goodreads. Goodreads can be partially theorized as an expression of 'the intimate public sphere' conceptualized by Lauren Berlant (1997). According to Berlant, the intimate public sphere is a 'juxtapolitical' (x) affective space in which participants experience a sense of social belonging through shared participation in consumer culture (viii). Goodreads is an ambiguous platform, neither entirely a social networking site nor merely a book reviewing site. Goodreads, therefore, is a productive site for considering how Heiss's literature contributes to broader social debate in that it provides a space for affective discussion centred around literature, and Heiss's readers are demonstrated to be diverse and differentiated.

This Element explores Heiss's own understanding and strategizing of writing into the genre of chick lit, as well as the diverse and differentiated reader expectations that have been brought to bear on her literature. Ultimately, the analysis undertaken throughout confounds academic understandings of the cogency of genre as an interpretative tool and presents new possibilities for future scholarship on chick lit.

2 The Author: Heiss's Position in the Australian Literary Field

In an interview conducted with the author, Anita Heiss referenced her own position in the Australian literary sphere. Querying established binaries, she stated, 'I think I'm still the only Aboriginal author that writes commercial fiction, as opposed to literary fiction . . . which is another debate because it's all fiction' (2017). Bourdieu argues that 'we cannot understand the significance of the actions of particular agents or organisations in literary culture until we understand the position they occupy' (1996: 85). Certainly at first glance, Heiss does not seem to inhabit a conventional authorial position within the literary field. Her chick lit novels achieved respectable sales figures, but were not breakout bestsellers.[5] On the other hand, and unlike most popular fiction, the novels have achieved some degree of literary consecration as reflected in their inclusion on a number of Australian university courses (Austlit, n.d.). Her presentation as an author of popular fiction is also informed by her work as an academic as her chick lit fuses the logic and practices of popular fiction with the ideas and concerns of her scholarship. According to Bourdieu, the literary field is a site of constant 'struggle' (1993: 184) as new positions within the field are constantly contested and re-negotiated. Heiss's movements between these positions – popular fiction and academia – are demonstrative of exactly this kind of authorial position creation. This section explores the success of this careful manoeuvring through Heiss's discussion of her writing practice, as well as critical reviews of her chick lit novels. Ultimately, the success of Heiss's strategizing is reflected in the diverse and differentiated reading publics that these reviews imply.

Heiss's decision to write in the genre of chick lit could be interpreted as a strategic and measured decision when considered in relation to her landmark study on the publishing industry as it relates to Indigenous authors, *Dhuuluu-Yala: To Talk Straight* (2003). In this text she clearly identifies systemic difficulties facing Indigenous authors publishing fiction works featuring Indigenous characters, issues, ideas and themes. Heiss argues that publishing houses often operate on the principle that texts by

---

[5] Thanks to NielsonBook Scan for assistance on determining sales figures.

Indigenous authors do not cohere with the tastes of the reading public. Instead publishers mistakenly assume that works by Indigenous authors are only of interest to Indigenous readers. Because of this assumption, Indigenous authors are not marketed in a way that would break this self-imposed cycle (94). She writes 'some publishers claim to have good marketing and distribution strategies, but admit there are areas that need developing so that the promotion of Aboriginal authors and their works is more rigorous and far-reaching' (90).

Heiss's criticism centres on the shortcomings of the mechanisms surrounding the promotion of Indigenous writing. In particular, the chapters 'Publishing the Indigenous Word' and 'Selling Indigenous Literature to the Reader' detail an industry assumption that 'the reading public is not interested in works by Aboriginal authors' (90). Heiss relates in detail her decision to self-publish her collection of poetry *Token Koori* (1998) following the disappointing royalties returned on her first publication, the satirical text *Sacred Cows* (1996): 'If you want your book to be out there, to be read, reviewed and appreciated, and hopefully bring in some of the estimated $3000 income that the average Australian author is supposed to get annually, then you have to do a lot more than just write it' (2003: 96). An awareness of the limitations of the market, potential pitfalls of one's chosen genre as well as an understanding that non-Indigenous readers will be largely the arbiters of success are highlighted as essential knowledge in the potential production of a highly marketable Indigenous text. Although the reception of texts by Indigenous authors has altered since the publication of *Dhuuluu-Yala*, what remains significant about Heiss's text is the way that she demonstrates expert understanding of the publishing industry as it relates to Indigenous authors and her ability to deploy this knowledge to situate herself in a mainstream genre. It is four years after the publication of *Dhuuluu-Yala* that Heiss then publishes the first of her chick lit novels.

Heiss is attracted to the chick lit genre on the basis that, in her words, 'I never saw women like myself in Australian fiction' (Heiss, 2017), that is, 'an urban, beachside Blackfella, a concrete Koori with Westfield Dreaming' (2012: 1). Heiss's PhD had emphasized the role of literature as a platform for activism and affirmation and celebration of Aboriginal culture. As she extrapolates in an interview in the *Sun Herald*:

> I did The Stolen Generations novel and that's done really
> well in schools [*The Diary of Mary Tallence*], but that was
> emotionally exhausting. I write lots of articles about
> Indigenous issues, identity and social justice. But there's
> other aspects to our lives as well and I wanted to write
> something that was funny. (Keenan, 2008)

Heiss's emphasis on lightness and humour coheres with her broader
political philosophy of writing. In particular, her writing challenges stereotypes of Indigenous women. She extrapolates:

> The whole point is to say, yes we do have careers in the
> Indigenous industry, or we teach Indigenous studies or
> whatever, but we have relationships. We fall in love, we
> fall out of love, we make love. That's about being a human
> being. It's not about being black and white. (Keenan, 2008)

Further, she is aware of a critical understanding of the genre as lower
status than other genres. Heiss recounts an early critical review of *Not
Meeting Mr Right* in which the reviewer, 'a middle class white guy' critiqued
the novel as 'formulaic' (Heiss, 2017). She responded to this criticism: 'Well
yes it is! Chick lit, or lots of writing is formulaic [but] it's how you use the
formula. For me it was how I used the formula to get the message across.
(Heiss, 2017)

In all of these quotations Heiss discusses genre authoritatively. Her
choice to write chick lit is articulated in explicitly strategic terms in
which genre is conceptualized as a sort of tool that is roughly capable of
achieving the distinct but joint aims of market success and dissemination
of empowering representations of Aboriginal women. Heiss's strategizing is explicitly reflected in an article published in the *Sun Herald*:
'[Heiss] has made no secret of the fact that her foray into chick lit has
been partly strategic. It is a conscious attempt to reach an audience that
wouldn't normally engage with Aboriginal issues and to offer an alternative view of what it means to be a contemporary Aboriginal woman'
(Fullerton, 2010).

2.1 Reviews from Newspapers and Literary Journals

In *Popular Fiction: the Logics and Practices of a Literary Field*, Gelder identifies genre as a point of distinction between literature and popular fiction: 'popular fiction announces those identities loudly and unambiguously', he writes, 'you know and need to know immediately that this is romance, or a work of crime fiction (and/or spy fiction), or science fiction, or fantasy, or horror, or a western, or an historical popular novel or an adventure novel' (42). In accordance with an understanding of popular fiction as a product produced for pleasure, Gelder further complicates the understanding of readers of popular fiction as passive and unreflexive: 'readers of popular fiction are careful discriminators of the field and careful readers of the work they process' (36). That is, to write in genre is key to writing a piece of popular fiction and any movement away from an established genre convention can be dangerous for authors relying on its established marketability. In addition to Steiner's definition of chick lit as 'fun, witty, easy and light reads dealing with real issues' (2008: par. 33), academic understandings of the genre emphasize the pursuit of a career, love and shopping as constitutive of the genre (Ferriss and Young, 2006; Harzewski, 2006, 2011; Merrick, 2006; Yardley, 2006). According to genre theory, Heiss's take on chick lit must theoretically strike a balance between the political dimension of her work focused on reclamation and celebration of identity and the focus on consumerism, career and dating essential to this genre.

Analysis of critical reviews of Heiss's chick lit provides a means of considering how her strategic positioning is interpreted and legitimated by cultural intermediaries, that is, individuals, groups or institutions that broadly mediate between the processes of the production and consumption of cultural products. They may be classified as 'taste-makers' in that they contribute to societal understandings of legitimate or consecrated culture (Fuller and Rehberg Sedo, 2013). Critical reviews of *Not Meeting Mr Right*, *Avoiding Mr Right*, *Manhattan Dreaming* and *Paris Dreaming* consistently define the novels as chick lit and highlight the political dimensions of the novels as a point of difference in genre. It is a point of emphasis in these reviews that *Not Meeting Mr Right* is the first piece of Aboriginal chick lit (Guivarra, 2007; Jaivin, 2007; Brunt, 2007). Further, reviews largely affirm

Heiss's discussed strategy to produce chick lit novels with a point of distinction. *Not Meeting Mr Right* is described as '[different] from typical chick lit in its "Blackfella" narrator Alice Aigner' (Becerra-Gurley, 2007: 187). Further, Kasey Brunt from *The Northern Territory News* writes, 'if you are thinking this book sounds like the hundreds of other chick lit titles flooding the market, think again' (2007). In both reviews, the emphasis on Aboriginal politics is identified as what distinguishes the novels from other chick lit.

While all reviews identify *Not Meeting Mr Right* as chick lit and emphasize the substantive nature of the subject matter, there is a division in terms of how well this dimension is perceived to be integrated. In a review for the academic journal *Antipodes*, Nicole Becerra-Gurley (2007) highlights this tension, 'Heiss' emphasis on the female Aboriginal perspective is the most thought provoking aspect of the novel; however, the way in which Heiss presents cultural issues detracts from the plot rather than enhances' (188). Despite this, Becerra-Gurley still concludes that, '*Mr Right's* enjoyment factor remains sufficient for reading in the bathtub or while relaxing at the beach' (188). Nancia Guivarra (2007) from *The Koori Mail*, however, identifies these argued moments of tension as constructive educative moments for the reader, writing, 'it is a rollicking good read, highly entertaining and for non-Indigenous readers in particular it has achieved a good balance of education about the issues Indigenous people face daily, with lashings of humour'. This position is shared by Kasey Brunt (2007) writing for the *Northern Territory News*: 'Heiss does tackle the usual issues about racism and identity in *Not Meeting Mr Right*. But she does it in an engaging – and funny – way.'

These criticisms and acclamations anticipate the reception of Heiss's subsequent chick lit novels. The emphasis on politics as a point of distinction in the genre is discussed as either inconsistent, incompatible with the rest of the story and explicitly didactic, or as successfully integrated and generative of teachable moments. Of *Paris Dreaming* Lorien Kaye (2011) from *The Age* writes, 'it's not that I disagree with any of Heiss' labored points, but her too-obvious agenda gets in the way of the story. And it's not a particularly gripping one at that.' Anne Fullerton (2010) from the *Sun Herald* reflects more favourably on *Manhattan Dreaming*:

the sub-genre of Australian Indigenous chick lit was virtually invented by Heiss and, in providing a more nuanced, accessible vision of Aboriginal identity, she has addressed a glaring absence from the literary landscape. The flipside of this is that the mechanics of the book are sometimes transparent and the novel's cultural education elements don't always blend easily with the narrative.

Critical reviews of Heiss largely reflect her own discussion of her strategic authorial practice as her novels are largely identified as chick lit with a point of difference; furthermore, these reviews assume a diverse and differentiated reading public inclusive of Aboriginal and settler Australians.

As one part of a broader apparatus of artistic consecration, critical reviews of Heiss's chick lit are instrumental in interpreting the strategy put forward by Heiss. Thus far, this discussion has drawn loosely on Bourdieusian terms and ideas to explore Heiss's presentation as an author of popular fiction. The remainder of this section, however, attends more closely to Bourdieu's sociology of literature. The value of this approach for Heiss is that his theory provides a way of conceptualizing the unique position that she inhabits in the Australian literary sphere. Specifically, his work provides a framework for exploring the complementary relationship Heiss establishes between academia and popular fiction. The next section attends more closely to Bourdieu's sociology of literature. Firstly, through a critical examination of his theoretical approach as it relates to Indigenous Australian authors. Secondly, I draw on Lahire's (2010) conception of the 'second job' (450) to explore how Heiss's academic career has supplemented and continues to inform her authorial identity and practice. Finally, I revisit Heiss's strategy within the context of the Australian publishing industry.

2.2 Bourdieu and the Sociology of Literature

As argued by Beth Driscoll, Bourdieu's theory of literary production provides 'a powerful, and flexible tool for understanding cultural behaviour' (2014: 12), and a number of academic texts have drawn on his work to produce comprehensive studies of literary cultures and industries (Radway,

1984; Tuchman and Fortin, 1989; Huggan, 2001; Casanova, 2004; Gelder, 2004; Driscoll, 2014; Dalleo, 2016). Bourdieu's sociology of literature is a three-tiered analysis: the locating of the literary field within the field of power; the positioning of agents within the literary field; and the tracing of the genesis of the author's habitus, that is, a culturally acquired collection of embodied practices, properties and dispositions that is generative of action and interpretations (Bourdieu, 1990: 53).

Bourdieu defines a field as a 'social universe' (1993: 164) governed by particular logics and practices. Society is made up of a number of different fields, including the field of economics, politics and of cultural production, of which the literary field is a subset. Each field is a site of struggle – analogized by Bourdieu as a 'game' (1993: 184) – that is stratified into two oppositional poles: the heteronomous (economic) and autonomous (symbolic), in which individual actor's compete for distinguishing forms of capital: economic, social, symbolic or cultural. The literary field is divided between the autonomous pole of 'art for art's sake' (1993: 182) also known as the field of restricted production, and the heteronomous pole of 'commercial art' (1996: 223) or the field of large-scale production. The latter includes popular writers who cater to a mass market.

The position that the author inhabits within any given field is informed by the individual's habitus, As argued by Jenkins (1992), the concept of habitus acts as a 'bridge building exercise' (74) between the extremes of subjectivism and objectivism in that it retains some understanding of individual agency – captured in the concept of dispositions – while also attending to broader deterministic structures in the form of the field. A mutual consideration of the literary field and the author's habitus produces a dynamic reading that illuminates the broader constitutive conditions of the role or position of the writer. Significantly, this approach partially accounts for the content of an author's literary production in that analysis of an author's position in the literary field illuminates 'what artists and writers can say or do' (Bourdieu, 1993: 166). Although the concept of habitus seeks to attend to an individual's agency and external structures in theorizing their actions the concept, nonetheless, runs the risk of flattening the dynamism and creativity of the author in question. With respect to Heiss, I am conscious that an uncritical application of the term perhaps encourages a reading that may reduce Heiss's identity as an Aboriginal woman to an essentialist understanding of identity. Some consideration of habitus remains necessary, however, and I retain a focus on language specific to the analysis of the field that is supplemented by Heiss's own discussion of her writing practice.

2.2.1 The Third Principle: Identity and Education

Motivated by prestige or wealth, Bourdieu's model of authorial action is largely individualistic and self-serving, eschewing the possibility for community-oriented and politically resistant art. In the postscript to *The Rules of Art* Bourdieu introduces the potential that literature can yield for political critique, an argument absent from his analysis in *The Field of Cultural Production*. He argues, however, that the power of a subfield is defined only by its 'disinterestedness', as the market 'places demands' on the author, which ultimately compromises any potential for critique. Autonomy, then, is defined by the capacity to resist these demands (Bourdieu, 1996: 217). Bourdieu's argument, thus, only consolidates an understanding of popular art and culture as not only artistically inferior, but also as ideologically suspect and compromised.

Bourdieu's theorization has recently been re-addressed, predominantly by scholars in postcolonial literary studies. This Element incorporates postcolonial literary theory as conducive with the Australian context. Although Australia is not a postcolonial nation, I follow the argument advanced by Nathaniel O'Reilly in *Post-colonial Issues in Australian Literature* (2010) that 'post-colonial reading strategies provide immensely productive ways for analysing Australian texts' (2). In the collection *Bourdieu and Post-colonial Studies* (2016) editor Raphael Dalleo emphasizes the potential that a Bourdieusian sociological approach yields for the study of postcolonial literature. In opposition to the 'high theory abstraction' (2) that is argued to dominate postcolonial studies, Dalleo suggests that Bourdieu offers a more grounded approach inclusive of the 'material nature' (2) of literary production. In a departure from dichotomy that Bourdieu establishes between art and the market, contributor Sarah Brouillette suggests that this relationship is in fact 'dialectical' (2016: 80), and not oppositional. She proposes that other forms of capital be theorized as animating agents within the literary field. Dalleo re-enforces this position and argues that postcolonial literature cannot be singularly interpreted as governed by either literary prestige or the mass market (8). As argued by Dalleo, 'postcolonial studies conceives of itself as not just seeking to interpret the world, but to change it' (8). That is, postcolonial literature is political in its most explicit sense, it is invested in the potential for political and social transformation.

Like Brouillette, Graham Huggan (2001) argues for a dialectical understanding of the literary field by suggesting that postcolonial authors are pulled between 'two principal regimes of value' (6): 'a politics of value that stands in obvious opposition to global processes of commodification' (6); and, 'a regime of value implicitly assimilative and market driven' (6). Outside postcolonial studies, Michel Hockx and Ivo Smits (2003), scholars of early modern Chinese literary culture, have also complicated Bourdieu's bipolaric understanding of the literary field to argue for the existence of a 'third principle' (225) that is largely community oriented: 'partly but not fully heteronomous, which motivates modern Chinese writers to consider as part of their practice, the well-being of their country and their people' (225). These interpretations of Bourdieu are significant as they advance the possibility of oppositional and critical writing – even in an increasingly or wholly commercial field.

It is clear that Heiss's literary practice cannot be schematized into the two conflicting principles definitive of Bourdieu's analysis of the French literary field. Heiss's discussions of her own writing practice partly reflect Huggan's definition of the postcolonial literary field in that she demonstrates a dual investment in a mass market readership, as well as – in the tradition of other Aboriginal authors – a desire for her literature to be political and socially transformative. This is demonstrated most coherently in a number of quotes taken from her memoir *Am I Black Enough For You?* (2012). Heiss's memoir was written partly in response to the racial discrimination lawsuit that Heiss and nine other Aboriginal Australians brought against journalist Andrew Bolt (Bolt Breached Discrimination Act, 2011).[6] Bolt was found to have

---

[6] The other individuals who sued Andrew Bolt included ATSIC chairman Geoff Clark, academic Professor Larissa Behrendt, activist Pat Eatock, photographer Bindi Cole, health worker Leeanne Enoch, native title expert Graham Atkinson, academic Wayne Atkinson and lawyer Mark McMillan (Bolt Breached Discrimination Act, 2011).

contravened section 18C of the Racial Discrimination Act through the publication of his articles, 'It's so hip to be black' (2009a), 'White is the new black' (2009b) and 'White fellas in the black' (2009c). These articles argued that 'fair-skinned' Aboriginal people were trading on their Aboriginal heritage for career reward and advantage (Bolt Breached Discrimination Act, 2011). Bolt wrote, 'I'm saying only that this self-identification as Aboriginal strikes me as self-obsessed, and driven more by politics than by any racial reality' (2009a). Heiss begins her memoir with a direct acknowledgement of her dual heritage, the focus of Bolt's attack, in order to intimately connect her authorial voice to her family and community:

> I aim to use my writing to reclaim pride in our status as First Nations people ... to use my published words as a vehicle for asserting my individual and communal identity, to instil pride in others, and to help non-Aboriginal people better understand us. I hope that, in turn, we can all then improve our under-standing of ourselves and our collective Australian identity. (6)

A second significant quotation comes later in the memoir: 'my strategy in choosing to write commercial women's fiction is to reach audiences that weren't previously engaging with Aboriginal Australia in any format, either personally, professionally or subconsciously. And it is that non-Indigenous female market that is key to my audience' (215). Heiss, thus, articulates the significance of her writing as dually an exercise in reclamation and celebra-tion of identity and as offering the possibility for producing social change through engagement with non-Indigenous Australians. This quote also encapsulates the idea of alternative forms of capital theorized by Hockx and Smits (2003). Heiss's discussion of her writing practice explicitly identifies the significance and value of literature as a tool for self-representation and definition underscored by an obligation and connection to community. Heiss also discusses her writing as a pedagogical tool: 'I want them to learn things, but I want all my books to teach in some way' (Heiss, 2017). But, her approach is more evocative of the language of reconciliation, with an emphasis on understanding, assistance and discus-sion, than it is bluntly didactic: 'I'm trying to create something that has a lasting life and will be used in classrooms to generate conversations and help people understand their role in society' (Heiss, 2017).

Heiss is connected to a long tradition of politically active Aboriginal writers. Literature (letters, petitions, poetry, painting) has consistently played a role in Aboriginal political resistance, self-definition and determination. In the collection *The Macquarie PEN Anthology of Aboriginal Literature* (2014), editors Anita Heiss and Peter Minter present the first collection of literature written in English by Aboriginal authors from the eighteenth century to the present. This collection not only presents a comprehensive history of 'Aboriginal literature' (2), but also more generally articulates a coherence of voice across 200 years, thus defining Aboriginal authorship as a 'practice and literary category' that represents 'the nexus between the literary and the political' (3). The history of Aboriginal writing may be summarized in the following distinct stages: letter writing; traditional stories; activist authors and poetry; and life writing. The history of letter writing includes those written by individuals to local authorities and newspapers and community-led petitions. Notable examples include Wangal man Bennelong's letter to 'Mr Philips, Steward to Lord Sydney' in 1792 and the Coranderrk petition (1886) compiled by Wurundjeri activist, diplomat and elder, William Barak – which petitioned against the closure of the Coranderrk settlement and advocated for Aboriginal rights to their own land. The history of traditional stories includes the work of Ngarrindjeri preacher, inventor and writer David Unaipon. His collection of traditional stories, *Native Legends* (1929) has been credited as the first publication by an Aboriginal author. In an era of assimilationist politics, Unaipon's collection represented the reclamation of pride in cultural practice. The history of activist writing and poetry includes Oodgeroo Noonucul's poetry collection *We are Going* (1967) that represented the beginning of a tradition of Aboriginal activist poetry. Noonucul's writing both informed and constituted her political activism. Poetry remains one of the most important genres in Aboriginal political and creative literature. Among many others, this includes: Lisa Bellear, Romaine Moreton, Gary Foley, Sam Watson and Jeanine Leanne. The history of life writing includes the autobiographical and testimonial fiction that characterized much of the writing of the 1980s and 1990s. Sally Morgan's *My Place* (1987), Doris Pilkington's *The Rabbit Proof Fence* (1996) and Ruby Langford Ginibi's

Don't Take Your Love to Town (1988) spoke back to a dominant historical narrative that disavowed violence perpetrated against Aboriginal Australians. Aboriginal literature today is diverse and multifaceted, and authors continue to expand into new genres and forms of storytelling. These include young-adult fiction (Ambelin Kwaymullini), science fiction (Ellen Van Neervan and Claire Coleman) and critically acclaimed literary fiction such as the novels by Miles Franklin award-winning authors Kim Scott and Alexis Wright. Bourdieu characterizes agents in the cultural field as 'dominated dominators', that is, they are structurally subordinate but with the symbolic power to legitimate or discredit the dominant group. As argued by Heiss and Minter, Aboriginal writing is characterized by 'the nexus between the literary and the political' (2014: 3). Contrary to Bourdieu's understanding of the literary field as demarcated between prestige and wealth, the history of Aboriginal writing is intimately connected to, and motivated by, social and political change. Explicitly, the power of Aboriginal writing has transcended the symbolic establishing it not only as a space for critique but also an instigator of political change.

The relationship between language and power is already well established in postcolonial studies as is the connection between language, identity and representation in Australian Indigenous studies. In *Textual Spaces: Aboriginality and Cultural Studies* (1992) Stephen Muecke argues that, 'Aboriginality is constructed in discourse' (19). Language produces the object of its reference and, historically, Aboriginal people have been textually constructed in three distinct discourses: the Anthropological; the Romantic; and the Racist (24). Each of these discourses objectifies, romanticizes and portrays Aboriginal people as non-normative and 'other'. Patrick Wolfe (2006) argues that colonization is not an event but a structure reinforced by the discourse and legitimating language of terra-nullius that excludes and marginalizes Aboriginal people (388). This denial of the right to Indigenous self-definition and determination operates as a mechanism of the logic that then upholds the structure of colonialism. Further, Marcia Langton's essay, *Well I Heard it on the Radio and Saw it on the Television* (1993), highlights a history of distorted and offensive representations of Aboriginal people in Australian film, and other cultural products, that operate to erase Aboriginal identity. Drawing on the work of E. Ann

Kaplan, Langton discusses how these representations produce an 'absence' of Aboriginal identity that is also constituted by its distorted 'presence' (24). Aboriginal literature is, thus, doubly an exercise in opposition and critique – an affront to colonial discourse – but also a site of cultural reclamation and pride. It is an intervention in a history of misrepresentation and bureaucratic categorization, and it is within this tradition that Heiss's literature is situated. Indeed, Heiss clearly articulates this herself, in 'Blackwords: writers on Identity' (2014), stating 'the act of writing often becomes more than solely creative for authors who use the process as a vehicle for analysing, understanding, asserting, determining and defining their own identity.'

2.2.2 The Second Job

In addition to contextualizing Heiss's writing within a tradition of Aboriginal literature, Heiss's academic work and career must also be considered as a significant part of her authorial persona. In 'The double life of writers' (2010) Bernard Lahire complicates Bourdieu's conception of the literary field that is arguably distinct from other fields owing to the dual membership of its participants. Most authors are plural actors who possess a 'second job' (45) in a distinct field that supplements their authorial practice. Lahire argues that field theory has been largely silent on the influence and significance of 'out of field practice' (447) as it relates to the literary field. Lahire's conception of the second job helps us understand Heiss's work in academia as entirely complementary and constitutive of her overall public profile. Heiss has moved between the academic and literary fields at different points in her career, sometimes participating in both simultaneously. While scholarship on genre acknowledges that the industry of popular fiction is partially defined by the public role of the author, who is intimately connected to their readership through quick turnaround of output, Heiss remains unusual in that her role as an academic and activist further characterizes her role as an author.

Throughout her career Heiss has been employed in a number of different occupations across the field of cultural production, politics and education. She has spent time, briefly, in the public service (Heiss, 2012: 100) and in independent arts organizations (Heiss, 2012: 44). Most consistently, however, her second job could be identified as her work in academia. In 2004 she was a part-time writer in residence at Macquarie University (Heiss, 2012: 114), between 2005 and 2006 she was Deputy Director of the Warawara Department of Indigenous Studies at Macquarie University, and she has also been employed as a full-time writer and Associate Professor at the Western Sydney University ('Anita's Career'). In 2017 she returned to academic work at the University of Canberra before assuming a professorship at the University of Queensland in 2018. Heiss's PhD dissertation, later published by Aboriginal Studies Press as *Dhuuluu-Yala: to Talk Straight – Publishing Indigenous Literature* (2003), established her as an authority on the Australian publishing industry as it relates to Aboriginal authorship. She has published extensively on literary criticism, predominantly in the Australian literary journals *Southerly*, *Meanjin* and *The Griffith Review*. She has also co-edited the collection *The Macquarie Pen Anthology of Aboriginal Literature* (2008) and composed the 'Blackwords Essays' for the online Australian literature database Austlit. Although Heiss writes in her memoir, 'I don't even consider myself an academic, even though I've jumped through all the hoops' (109), in public appearances and presentations she is acknowledged and introduced as Dr Anita Heiss. Her past and present institutional affiliations, PhD in literature and substantial publication history contribute significantly to her authorial identity as she translates the cultural capital of academia into the broader literary field.

The relationship between the literary and academic fields is of great significance when considering Aboriginal literature. For Heiss, there is a homology between the principles that motivate her work in the literary and academic fields. Heiss reflects on the research behind her PhD as being driven by a desire to 'give a voice to Aboriginal Australian literature, because I wanted students in the future to be able to quote us, and not just another white academic' (Heiss, 2012: 107). Heiss emphasizes the significance of the production of scholarship by Aboriginal Australians in countering a tradition of objectifying and racist scholarship. The aforementioned quote not only reflects the significance of self-representation, but also more broadly acknowledges the importance of doing this within the academic field in that universities are sites of knowledge creation and education. Accordingly, Heiss has discussed universities as sites of consecration and legitimation of Aboriginal literature. In an interview conducted with the author, Heiss said:

I had a conversation with a poet recently who is quite down
on academia and said you know: 'it hasn't done anything for
me,' and I had to say, 'you need to stop saying that, because
there are people working in universities who are teaching
your work.' And you go and have a look, and you know, if
you win an award it is usually a university award and you
know universities they're probably the biggest buyers of your
books and are actually reading them and talking about them.
So you can criticize universities but that's where the conversations are happening, particularly with poetry, it's not happening in book clubs necessarily or on the beach. (2017)

Accordingly, although Heiss's fiction publications outwardly position her
as an author of popular fiction at the heteronomous pole of the literary
field, she has a certain status within the education system. Within the
academic field, Heiss's chick lit novels have been taught at the University
of Newcastle, the University of Wollongong, and Macquarie University
between 2011 and 2015 (Austlit, n.d.).

Heiss, however, does identify limitations with the academic context at
a personal and collective level with respect to the promotion and advocacy
of Indigenous affairs. She reiterates a conception of the academy as
divorced and distinct from 'the real world' (2012: 105). In her memoir she
reflects on the insularity of the academic community as well as its remove
from the politics that it ostensibly promulgates. She writes, 'I never understood the point of academics talking purely to academics when those in the
"real" world needed and wanted to engage as well' (2012: 131). Here, Heiss
is not only identifying the exclusionary and elitist nature of academic
practice and institutions, but also the need for academics to take their
knowledge to the public. The language of academic discourse plays
a large part in this. Heiss discusses the peculiarity of the efforts to define
Aboriginality that only 'alienated' (2012: 131) those who were the object of
this enquiry. Heiss identifies her position in academia as 'privileged',
underscored by the responsibility to take knowledge back to the broader
mainstream and Indigenous community: 'I need to use my position and my
privilege to help others in the community make the most of the rights our

peoples have fought for' (Heiss, 2012: 14). It was within this context, however, that Heiss gained both the skills and some industry connections to begin to establish her career as a fiction author. While finishing her PhD at UNSW she was invited by Scholastic to publish a children's book that would eventually become *Who Am I? The Diary of Mary Talence* (2001). In this case the structured nature of her academic training provided the basis for the publication of her first novel: 'it was actually a really good way of moving into writing fiction because it was a very simple format . . . so I was given the structure, given the word length, I was given the age of character and the reading audience. So all I had to do was write the story with all these guidelines (Heiss, 2017). Following this publication Heiss expanded into the genre of chick lit with the publication of *Not Meeting Mr Right*.

2.3 Which Comes First: the Genre or the Cover?

Although Heiss speaks authoritatively about her chosen genre she is not always entirely consistent in her rationalization of genre as strategic practice. In an interview conducted with the author, for example, Heiss partially attributes the inspiration for *Not Meeting Mr Right* to reading Georgia Blain's *Closed for Winter* (1998), Rosie Scott's *Movie Dreams* (1995) and *Glory Days* (1988) and Linda Jaivin's works. Reflecting on these novels she states, 'I never saw women like myself in Australian fiction . . . I don't know where the original idea came from; but I had this idea of wanting to do these dates from hell . . . and that was *Not Meeting Mr Right*' (2017). Although authors such as Linda Jaivin are largely classified as authors of chick lit, Heiss goes on to assert that 'I never read chick lit, I didn't know I was writing chick lit until I met with my publisher at the time' (Heiss, 2017). She further states in the same interview, 'I'd started my first chick lit novel – which I didn't know was chick lit' (Heiss, 2017). In this interview, Heiss seemingly discusses genre in a less explicitly strategic manner. Genre is inspiration but is not explicitly identifiable. With respect to her first chick lit novel, *Not Meeting Mr Right*, she suggests that the classification of the novel as chick lit only occurred after it was completed and was something that was determined by her publisher. As Heiss explains:

> I didn't know I was writing chick lit, I just wanted to write
> this story, but [it's] the sales and marketing departments that

determine the genre because they're the ones who have to go
into the bookshops to sell them. (Heiss, 2017)

Heiss further recounts the significance of certain paratextual elements in
establishing the genre for *Not Meeting Mr Right* and her subsequent novels.
Genette and Maclean (1991) argue that a book is much more than 'a lengthy
sequence of verbal utterances more or less containing meaning' (261).
A book's 'para-textual' elements, such as an author's name, a title, a preface
or illustrations are 'the means by which a text makes a book of itself and
proposes itself as such to readers' (261). For chick lit this is particularly
important with scholars identifying the distinctive pastel-coloured covers as
the genre's 'identikit' (Harzewski, 2011: 2). Heiss recalls the process of the
design of *Not Meeting Mr Right*'s book cover and the explicit connection
between design and designation of genre. The process of the design involved
sending the synopsis and fifteen of the year's bestselling novels in that genre
to the designer. She quotes her publisher's instructions to the designer, 'here's
the story, make it look something like that' (Heiss, 2017).

As much as Heiss speaks of strategy regarding writing into genre, her
account of the writing and then marketing of *Not Meeting Mr Right*
indicates that genre was largely imposed at the level of the marketing
of the book. In this case, the cover design provided a strong frame for
presenting *Not Meeting Mr Right*, and its subsequent novels, as chick lit.
Heiss expands on this conversation with her publisher: 'The women who
buy these books know what they are looking for, they'll go in the shop
and they don't know specifically the title of the author [but] they will
look for a book that looks like the one they just read' (Heiss, 2017).
Although Heiss does at times position the development of *Not Meeting
Mr Right* as strategic, her concession that she 'didn't know [she] was
writing chick lit' (Heiss, 2017) does highlight the extent to which the
publisher's marketing of the text was a significant factor in determining
the genre of the novel. For *Not Meeting Mr Right*, chick lit was seemingly
imputed after the fact.

The apparent inconsistencies between Heiss's unawareness of chick lit
and also the argument that she 'uses' the genre, need not be contradictory.
Although there is some inconsistency in the way that Heiss discusses chick

lit, she is resoundingly consistent in her discussion of the associated genre of commercial women's fiction:

> It is that non-Indigenous female market that is key to my audience: let's face it, there are not enough Blackfellas to sustain any publishing venture, least of all an entire genre. With this in mind, I made a conscious decision to move into the area of commercial women's fiction, releasing four books in the genre of 'chick lit' or, as friends at Koorie Radio 93.7 FM categorized it, 'choc-lit'. (2012: 215)

Heiss seems to make a critical distinction between commercial women's fiction and chick lit. At another point in our interview Heiss discusses genre as a strategic tool: 'I appreciate that genre is about targeting . . . a particular audience' (Heiss, 2017). Heiss explicitly considers commercial women's fiction as connected to a mainstream audience, a point extended in the interview: 'I'd made this conscious decision to reach this broad audience of Australian women who are on the bus or at the beach or in books clubs who may never have read a book by an Aboriginal author before' (Heiss, 2017). In Heiss's discussion, commercial women's fiction is a vehicle that allows the writer to take a political message to the broadest possible audience:

> It's not about the sales . . . well, it is about the sale! For every sale someone is reading it, and so I go 'how do I take a message about black deaths in custody or the NT intervention or cultural appropriation and make it palatable or relatable in an everyday story for Australian women to read?' (Heiss, 2017)

Commercial women's fiction, thus, in Heiss's retrospective theorization is an already distinguished general category that presents relatable and palatable stories to an audience of Australian women who read for leisure. It is about targeting a specific reader. The consolidation then of Heiss's first novel, *Not Meeting Mr Right*, from commercial women's fiction to chick lit appears largely as a refinement and qualification made by the publishing house for matters of marketing. Heiss articulates the conscious positioning of her second novel as consolidating the authorial position established by *Not Meeting Mr Right*: 'I went to do *Avoiding Mr Right* and chose to set it in Melbourne, because I was very conscious of markets and audiences' (Heiss, 2017). Further, 'the first one was about pioneering the Koori chick-lit genre … so this one [*Avoiding Mr Right*] was really about wanting to establish my name in the genre. The market's flooded with chick stories and I wanted it to be distinctly different, so it has got indigenous politics etc' (Keenan, 2008). The publication of *Not Meeting Mr Right* demonstrated the viability of Heiss's chick lit. The subsequent three novels were then developed closely in alignment with this new designation of genre. Heiss demonstrates an awareness and emphasis on the importance of genre from the moment she began writing *Not Meeting Mr Right*. Genre, however, became a more explicit and coherent strategic measure following the refinement of the novel as chick lit by her publisher.

Critical reviews of Heiss largely reflect Heiss's own discussion of her strategic authorial practice as her novels are largely identified as chick lit with a point of difference. Heiss's desire to write chick lit is articulated in explicitly strategic terms in which genre is conceptualized as a sort of tool roughly capable of achieving the distinct but joint aims of market success and dissemination of empowering representations of Aboriginal women. Genre, however, is something only approximately theorized by the author and is further refined and consolidated by the publisher. Section 3 will extend this discussion to incorporate academic understandings of chick lit that are more rigidly defined. In opposition to this approach I propose a reader-based response as a way of complementing analysis of the literary field.

3 The Page: Genre, Formula and a Turn to the Reader

Scholarship on chick lit seeks to address the marginalization of the genre by arguing its importance as a source of socio-cultural commentary. Analysis is largely conducted through ideological reading of the novels and discussion of adherence or deviation from a formulaic understanding of chick lit. In this section I uphold the importance of an ideological approach to reading chick lit that focuses on Heiss's depiction of a nascent Aboriginal middle class. I argue, however, that a strictly ideological approach is not sufficient to capture the complexity of these novels. Through a comprehensive review of scholarship on chick lit I explore how this approach, supplemented by a formulaic understanding of genre, can cast novels by women of colour as either deviations or subversions of the prototypical chick lit novel. Through a consideration of Anne Brewster's interpretation of Martin Nakata's theory of 'the cultural interface', and an understanding of genre as a 'fuzzy' and 'historically contingent' organizational practice (Frow, 2006: 80), I propose a reader-response approach as a way of circumventing some of the limitations of contemporary scholarship on chick lit.

3.1 Definition, Origin and Significance of Chick Lit

Academic and industry understandings of the genre present the pursuit of a career, love and shopping as uniformly constitutive of chick lit. That is, through first-person narration, an urban-based woman heavily invested in consumer culture 'comes of age' or 'consciousness' through episodes of dating (Yardley, 2006: 4). Since its inception – heralded by the publication of *Bridget Jones's Diary* (1996) – the genre has been lambasted for its frivolity and superficiality. In 2001, Booker Prize nominee Beryl Bainbridge denounced the genre as 'a froth sort of thing' concerned with 'helpless girls, drunken, worrying about their weight and so on' (quoted in Ferriss and Young, 2006: 1). A lack of profundity or originality is a common critique, and the title of chick lit has become so offensive to some that anthologies have even been compiled in opposition to the term. *This is Not Chick Lit* (2006) edited by Elizabeth Merrick is a compilation of women's short fiction, that is emphatically not chick lit. Merrick defines the genre in the following terms:

Chick lit is a genre, like a thriller, the sci-fi novel, or the
fantasy epic. Its form and content are, more or less formulaic: white girl in the big city searches for Prince Charming,
all the while, shopping, alternately cheating on or adhering
to her diet, dodging her boss, and enjoying the occasional
teary-eyed lunch with her token Sassy Gay friend. (vii)

Merrick and Bainbridge dismiss the genre of chick lit on the grounds of
its supposed frivolity and superficiality. A modest number of advocates,
however, refute this and argue for the genre's substantive nature based on
its historical affiliations and cultural significance. Novels such as Jane
Austen's *Pride and Prejudice* (1813) are argued to be a precursor to the
genre owing to their interrogation of societal norms, focus on marriage and
partnering, and wry witty humour (Ferriss and Young, 2006: 5). Other
feminist scholars have cautioned against superficial criticism that dismisses
the texts on the basis of their affiliation with consumer culture; an argument,
they point out, that dates back to the very beginning of female authorship.
Stephanie Harzewski (2006), a dominant force in chick lit scholarship,
explains the genre's significance:

Chick lit . . . responds to upheavals in the dating and mating
order through a mixed strategy of dramatization, farce and
satire. Daughters of educated baby boomers, chick lit heroines, in their degree of sexual autonomy and professional
choices stand as direct beneficiaries of the women's liberation movement. Yet they shift earlier feminist agendas, such
as equal pay for equal work, to lifestyle concerns. Unlike
earlier generations, chick protagonists and their readers
have the right to choose; now the problem is too many
choices. (37)

That is, chick lit represents contemporary gender politics post women's
liberation exemplified by the paradoxical tyranny and freedom of choice.
They reflect the complexities of contemporary life as women seek to
reconcile competing demands for autonomy and recognition in the

workplace and the desire for monogamous and fulfilling personal relationships. On this topic, Ferriss and Young argue for a sense of 'authenticity' (2006: 4) implicit in this new form. Unlike the high romance novels that preceded it, chick lit has aspirations to reflect the lived reality of modern urban women (2006: 4). Authenticity is associated with the confessional form expressed through the use of letters and emails that craft the impression that the protagonist is speaking directly to its readers (2006: 4). As argued by Nora Séllei, this assists in the identification of the reader with the protagonist that is a key factor in the genre's success (175).

Bridget Jones's Diary (1996) is widely discussed as pioneering the genre, although this genealogy is now contested (Hurt, 2018b; Valenzuela, 2018). The novel's success is attributed to Bridget's self-effacing, wry and witty commentary expressed through the intimate and confessional form of diary entries. In this form, Bridget externalized the anxieties of first-world womanhood characterized by an obsession with weight, alcohol and men. *Bridget Jones's Diary* inspired a prolific number of copycat novels that, in the words of Rosalind Gill and Elena Herdieckerhoff (2006), 'centred on the life of a thirty-something female who was unhappily single, appealingly neurotic, and preoccupied with the shape, size and look of her body, and with finding a man' (89). The novel was significant not only for its articulation of a new fictional style, but also for its expression of a distinctively post-feminist sensibility that is described in the following terms (489):

> Chick lit articulates a distinctively post-feminist sensibility characterized by an emphasis on neo-liberal feminine subjectivities and self-surveillance and monitoring; the notion of the (sexual) body as the key source of identity for women; discourses of boldness, entitlement, and choice (usually articulated to normative femininity and/or consumerism); and a belief in the emotional separateness of men's and women's worlds. It is also characterised by an entanglement of feminist and anti-feminist discourses. (1)

Post-feminist politics, as expressed in chick lit, is marked unambiguously by a sense of contradiction and inconsistency. Consequently, this hypocrisy, ambiguity and confusion operates as an implicit commentary on the gains and deficiencies of second-wave feminism (Harzewski, 2011: 2). Scholarship on the area stresses the significance of these texts as cultural products that further illuminate the reality of late capitalism and the way that the commercial has infiltrated the personal. The contradiction and inconsistencies of the protagonist's politics are, therefore, reflections of this complexity.

3.2 Chick Lit and Race: Room for Difference?

The first critical collection on chick lit, *Chick Lit: The New Woman's Fiction* (2006) appeared a decade after the publication of *Bridget Jones's Diary*. Initially, critical focus was centred on British or American novels and the genre was understood to be widely ethnocentric; marketed to attract and featuring single, urban-based, white women in their twenties and thirties (Gill and Herdieckerhoff, 2006: 1). In 2008 Pamela Butler and Jigna Desai argued for greater attention to be paid to chick lit written by women of colour, until then notably absent from the field. In this section I provide an overview of the development of this scholarship in order to suggest an alternative analytic approach based on reader response.

In her article '"Sistahs are doin' it for themselves": chick lit in black and white' (2006) Lisa Guerrero analyses the distinction between chick lit and sistah lit, a subgenre of the form that portrays African American protagonists. Guerrero argues for a critical distinction between the two forms. Sistah lit is distinct in that its protagonists must fight racial as well as gendered barriers in their search for self-actualization. Where the women of chick lit are characterized by monogamous coupling and the promise of domesticity, the women of sistah lit – informed by a history that connected African American female identity to histories of forced compliance with the roles of caretaker, breeder and sexualized object – reject this containment within a domestic setting (90). Guerrero identifies Terry McMillan's *Waiting to Exhale* (1992) as a precursor of the genre that would influence and establish the marketability for authors Pearl Cleage and April Sinclair.

Ferriss and Young, however, argue that more recent black chick lit or sistah lit lacks the political fervour of McMillan's work and, 'studiously avoid references to racial inequality or specifically black problems or concerns' (2006: 8). This position is similarly expressed in a *New York Times* article by Lola Ogunnaike published two years earlier; Oggunaike argues that more recent black chick lit tends to be neither racially charged nor didactic: 'The protagonists, educated and decidedly middle to upper class, effortlessly mingle with both black and white characters. Love, not privilege, is the only real speed bump.' Novels such as *The Accidental Diva* (2001), *Bling* (2004), *Gotham Diaries* (2004) and *FAB: A Novel* (2006), feature protagonists not struggling with race but only with their fabulous careers.

Amanda Maria Morrison (2010), similarly questions the problematic representation of the Latina woman in Alisa Valdes-Rodriguez's literature and reaches a similar conclusion to Ferriss and Young. *The Dirty Girls Social Club* (2003), written by Valdes-Rodriguez, was the first novel by a Latina author to debut on the *New York Times* bestseller list and is considered to be the originator of the subgenre of Chicana chick lit. The novel features the friendship of American women of different racial and ethnic backgrounds who find common ground due to their mutual Latina heritage. Morrison argues that although superficially the novel appears to affirm the identities and culture of Latin American women, the women are only united around a bourgeois sensibility characteristic of chick lit – focussed on career aspirations, body consciousness and conspicuous consumption – which bears no correlation to the particularity of their Latin American identities.

Subgenres of chick lit, especially those attendant to issues of race and identity such as sistah lit and chica lit, cannot be discussed as homogenous wholes. Each subgenre is respectively characterized by racial and cultural specificities and histories. In discussing these subgenres, I do not intend to collapse the differences between the two, thereby designating perhaps some kind of 'minority' chick lit. What is significant in the critiques of Ferriss and Young (2006), Morrison (2010) and Oggunaike (2004), however, is the shared emphasis on the exclusion of racial politics from recent expressions of these genres. The question they cumulatively pose is where does race feature in contemporary chick lit? Such an observation does not seek to reduce the identity of the author to that singularly of race or ethnicity; we should ask in equal measure why a focus on race should be considered a missing component of these novels at all? Or in the case of Morrison's critique of Valdez-Rodriguez, what would it mean to produce a more 'authentic' representation of Latin American women? Tia Williams provides some insight when discussing her novel, *The Accidental Diva* (2001): 'Recent black fiction has been full of whiny, suffering-from-hair-politics, my-man-done-me-wrong women. Sounds pat, but many people still think you need to be downtrodden to be truly black' (quoted in Ogunnaike 2004). Williams, therefore, situates her novel as expressive of new formations of African American subjectivities.

Despite the language of Ferriss and Young (2006), Morrison (2010) and Oggunaike (2004), race has always been a component of chick lit. For example, *Bridget Jones's Diary* details the life of a thirty-something-year-old white British woman and although the text has been largely read with relation to emergent post-feminist female subjectivities, it is equally a narrative about what it means to be a young, white woman in Britain. The criticisms presented by Ferriss and Young, Oggunaike, and Morrison emphasize that protagonists of sistah lit and chica lit do not discuss their racial or ethnic identities in any explicit terms: race remains a large component of the literature; however, it is sublimated with respect to other formative aspects of identity. Cumulatively, these critics express the idea that the overarching politics of the genre, primarily the investment in consumerism, overrides and sublimates the politics attendant to race and cultural specificity.

In scholarship, attendance to these elements pursues the question, 'What does race and cultural specificity *do* to the genre?' The conclusions drawn are largely pessimistic. Perhaps this is the wrong question to ask. A more productive approach may be to consider the articulation of distinct feminisms as expressed by diverse cultural and racial groups, thereby acknowledging the intersectionality of race and gender. In their article 'Manolos, marriage and mantras: chick lit criticism and transnational feminism' (2008), Pamela Butler and Jigna Desai highlight the limitations of scholarship on chick lit. Butler and Desai argue that scholarship focusses on gender and sexuality around the nexus of personal choice. The absence of consideration of race reinforces the white woman as the genre's protagonist and subsequently has produced criticism that reductively reads women of colour as either identical to or a derivative of this assumed norm (4). This approach erases difference and does not acknowledge distinctions in different articulations of feminism. Butler and Desai supplant a focus on post-feminism with that of neo-liberal feminisms, described as the 'shift from liberal concern with state-ensured rights to a neoliberal politics understood through the notion of "choice"' (8). In so doing they draw attention to broader structural inequalities omitted from former analysis. Contrary to scholarship that identifies the problematic contradictory and paradoxical politics of the genre – an argument synonymous with post-feminism – Butler and Desai argue that their chosen novels of analysis are keenly aware of the problematics of neo-liberalism. In fact, protagonists of these novels employ these logics to produce potential spaces of resistance in which identity can be re-imagined (9).

Written in 2009, Cecilia Conchar Farr's chapter 'It was chick lit all along: the gendering of a genre', details the development of scholarship on chick lit. In an effort to situate the genre as serious literature, Farr identifies the dominance of what she terms 'a cultural approach' inclusive of: historical analysis; the association of chick lit with women's writing; and social commentary (202). This approach operates to situate the genre as a viable object of analysis, through attention to the novels' relationship to second-wave feminism, rather than through the conventional literary approach of attention to aesthetic standards. This approach, however, is problematic for two reasons. Firstly, the desire to identify the feminist credentials of the genre within the context of second-wave feminism invariably produces circular conclusions. While some critics identify the genre as progressive (Benstock, 2006; Mabry, 2006) it is more common to see ambiguous conclusions drawn (Gill and Herdieckierhoff, 2006; Umminger, 2006; Rowntree et al., 2012). As Farr argues, positioning the analysis of chick lit exclusively around what I term ideological analysis significantly limits the possibilities of interpretation. This approach has produced overwhelmingly negative or ambiguous conclusions that further marginalize the genre and recast it as trivial and problematic. As expressed by Farr, 'with this dominant approach to chick lit, consumerism reinforces sexism, and the take home message of the novels, the critics conclude, is that to buy things, to fix yourself, if you are lucky you will be rewarded with romance' (2009: 204).

Secondly, the taxonomy of genre engineered in scholarship is illusory. Farr points out that Terry McMillan's *Waiting to Exhale* (1992) is often excluded from the category of chick lit. Despite displaying many of the constitutive elements of the genre, the novel is bypassed for *Bridget Jones's Diary*, and is instead only discussed as its precursor. This continues what Farr describes as 'the regrettable move to "whiten" a tradition when we want to subject it to scholarly analysis' (2009: 203). Farr argues that this is largely the result of connecting the genre to canonical classics that are argued to be early examples of the genre. Consistently, various scholars retroactively identify *Pride and Prejudice* (1813) as chick lit (Séllei, 2006; Harzewski, 2011).

Both manoeuvres operate to legitimate the genre as serious literature but in so doing further potentially marginalize and flatten its complexity. In 2011 Harzewski called for further scholarship to be written on non-Western focused chick lit (17) and in the last couple of years there has been an explosion of scholarship in this area with articles and collections focussing on India (Malik, 2019; Bharti, 2019; Meyer, 2018), South Africa (Fasselt, 2019; Spencer, 2019), Uganda (Spencer, 2019), the French-Afro diaspora (Moji, 2018; Gehrmann, 2019) and Latin America (Valenzuela, 2018), amongst others. Significantly, much of this writing moves away from the previously predominant post-feminist approach, thereby avoiding the pitfalls of identifying the genre as either progressive or regressive.

An early example of this argument was advanced by Eva Chen (2010) who called on scholars to move away from a value-based appraisal of the genre towards an approach that accommodates the genre's inner tensions and layers. Aïda Valenzuela (2018) and Lucinda Newns (2018) apply the framework of neo-liberalism to undermine readings that interpret non-white chick lit as inauthentic or problematic. In opposition to earlier scholarship, such as Morrison's (2010) argument that Alisa Valdes-Rodriguez's *Dirty Girls Social Club* only presents a somewhat superficial representation of Latina identity, Valenzuela argues that such novels 'balance awkwardly' (8) the rejection of staid racialized and classed stereotypes and the integration of a defined Latin American identity into the rubric of American values. These novels, thus, are representative of major socio-economic changes in the late and early twenty-first century in the USA and speak to the conditions that legitimate cultural citizenship.

Newns argues that the chick lit novels of British Muslim authors Leila Aboulela and Shelina Zahra Janmohamed subvert the genre to instil the Western secular form of the novel with an Islamic worldview. In these novels, the definitive and neo-liberal narrative of self-discovery is reframed, then, as a journey towards God (2018: 295). Ankita Malik (2019) pursues a similar line of enquiry in her writing on Indian Chick Lit but instead focusses on the concept of the Consumer Society as articulated by Baudrillard to explore the way in which these novels speak to the development of cultural globalization while also attending to the cultural specificity of their locale.

This critical departure, however, does not wholly represent the demise of a mode of analysis partially focused on considering the progressive/regressive values of the novels. Lynda Gichanda Spencer (2019) applies a transnational, African feminism and post-feminist frame to explore the 'double-bind' of protagonists in the novels of Goretti Kyomuhendo, Zukiswa Wanner and Cynthia Jele. And, Erin Hurt, in the edited collection *Theorizing Ethnicity and Nationality in the Chick Lit Genre* (2018a), presents these narratives as neo-liberal fairy-tales that, 'do not accommodate inequality on a social and cultural level' (2018a: 15). Other approaches, such as that expressed by Polo Belina Moji (2018) take a completely different approach and employ hip-hop feminist theory and critical cultural analysis of black visuality to explore the novels of French author Lauren Ekué.

This new wave of chick lit scholarship, focused on non-white articulations of the genre, goes some way towards redressing the criticism levelled by Farr regarding the state of scholarship in 2009. In addition to a movement away from post-feminism, Erin Hurt and Aïda Valenzuela (2018) both imagine a genealogy that takes *Waiting to Exhale*, not *Bridget Jones's Diary*, as the genre's point of origin.

Farr argues that a cultural approach, or ideological analysis, sidestepped the demands of aesthetic analysis to legitimate chick lit as a viable object of study. I would add to this that the formalization and codification of chick lit as an identifiable genre in scholarship was of equal necessity and remains present in contemporary writings on chick lit. Qualification and definition of the genre achieved a number of general aims:

- It annexed chick lit from general romance and unified an identifiable corpus. This identification allowed scholars to argue that chick lit represented a new and culturally significant literary phenomenon.
- A genre-based approach focused on identifying and analysing its constitutive discursive and thematic elements also presented an alternative to a more traditional aesthetic literary approach.
- It allowed scholars to connect the genre with its literary antecedents, namely *Pride and Prejudice*, thereby further advancing the argument for merit by association.

The issue with this approach is that this earlier theorization was advanced around Anglo representations of the genre. Erin Hurt (2018b), in a chapter which reimagines a taxonomy of chick lit that originates with *Waiting to Exhale*, reflects: 'Scholars' analyses, including Ferriss and Young, Harzewski, Heike Mißler, and my own, as well as many others, have been limited by a focus on those historical or cultural conditions or tropes that easily connect to the white protagonist in *Bridget Jones's Diary* or those in the other white chick lit that closely followed Fielding' (161).

Despite recent advances, scholarship on chick lit still defers to an idea of the 'proto-typical' (Montoro 2012: 17) or 'traditional' (Mathew 2016a: 1) articulation of the genre defined by white protagonists. When this approach is applied to non-white chick lit it has a propensity to recast it as derivative of, or as I argue, a deviation, transformation or subversion of the proto-typical or traditional genre formation. As argued by Guerrero in her discussion of sistah lit, the protagonists of non-white articulations of chick lit must surmount both gendered and racialized barriers. An argument that understands chick lit to be singularly defined by gendered barriers may simply interpret the added dimension of race as implicitly political. Thereby politicizing identity, not representation.

3.3 A Tradition Continued: Scholarship on Heiss

A similar approach is evident in the small body of scholarship written on the subject of the chick lit of Anita Heiss. Imogen Mathew (2016a) argues that *Not Meeting Mr Right* destabilizes the genre of chick lit. An argument for destabilization implies that there is first a stable expression of the genre.

Although Mathew does not explicitly identify this, she does argue that there is a traditional articulation of the genre: 'The chick lit genre is hetero-normative, white, and middle class, traditional gender binaries are taken seriously and living the big city, consumer culture dream shapes the narrative arc' (1). By foregrounding 'a non-Western, non-white subjectivity' (1) Heiss is argued to be participating in an act of 'subversion' and 'resistance' (3). Despite this identification, Mathew's argument remains centred on the perceived identification of destabilization. According to Mathew, destabilization means that Heiss's attention to racial politics in the novel intensifies its hetero-normativity. She writes, 'by altering one variable, other features of the genre take on a sharper (and in this case, more conservative and more humorous) cast' (6).

Lauren O'Mahoney (2018) argues that Heiss both innovates and broadens the genre in her representation of Indigenous women navigating romantic, professional and cultural scenarios (42). She explores textual strategies in Heiss's writing aimed at raising consciousness in readers about Aboriginal Australian peoples (54). Although O'Mahoney does concede that the genre is not a self-evidently stable category (42) her analysis is conducted in accordance with a genealogy of the genre that understands *Bridget Jones's Diary* as its originary point and prototypical articulation.

Wenche Ommundsen (2011), author of the article 'Sex and the global city: chick lit with a difference', argues in accordance with the aforementioned critics on race and chick lit (Oggunaike, 2004; Ferriss and Young, 2006; Morrison, 2010), that Heiss's politics are 'blunted' (2011: 119) by the genre convention of chick lit itself. Ommundsen's article is significant in that she applies a transnational framework to focus on the diversity of and different articulations of cosmopolitanisms in chick lit novels from China, Saudi Arabia and Australia. Despite this, Ommundsen's analysis still recasts chick lit that features a non-white protagonist as coming up short. Heiss's main point, she argues, is to defy stereotypes, including that of the angry activist. Her books suggest that it is possible to be committed to Aboriginal politics without forgoing the pleasures of romance and consumer culture. She writes, 'it is a message to which her target readership – presumably less accustomed to, and less tolerant of, a more activist style of writing – is likely to be receptive.

But it does blunt her politics, reducing debates about both race and gender to relatively "safe" issues related to lifestyle and identity' (119).

Demonstrated in the analyses of Mathew and Ommundsen is a conception of genre that accords greater power to the implicit formula of genre rather than the author herself. Indeed, Mathew's conclusion that 'using the chick lit genre to promulgate an explicitly political message is, perhaps inevitably, an exercise in compromise' (2016a: 9) coheres with broader criticism that suggests the genre struggles to incorporate politics distinct from its 'traditional' articulation (Oggunaike 2004: Ferriss and Young 2006; Morrison 2010). Perhaps because the identity of Heiss's protagonists resists a reading focused exclusively around second-wave feminism, scholarship focused on her novels reveals some inconsistencies regarding the relationship of the genre convention of chick lit to her novels. For example, Mathew primarily argues that Heiss 'destabilises' the genre, but then also that she 'appropriates it' (2016a: 1). Further, she suggests that the genre 'suggests a plasticity' (2016a: 1) that can incorporate non-white protagonists, but that alteration in the genre's variables reproduces its conservatism. In this case, Mathew argues that *Not Meeting Mr Right* presents a subtle undercurrent of homophobia that is largely the product of alteration in the genre's variables. Cumulatively, these scholars suggest that deviation from the perceived formula results in a profoundly problematic text. The author ultimately remains entirely constrained by the perceived limits of the genre.

3.4 Ideological Analysis and Mapping of Heiss's Chick Lit

A genre-based approach, and the ideological approach outlined by Farr can be limiting when applied to non-white articulations of the genre. Section 1 explored the strategic practice of Heiss in writing into the genre of chick lit, but this cannot be discussed entirely independently of any consideration of the narratives of the novels. This section undertakes a reading of the novels inspired by the intersectional approach encouraged by Butler and Desai (2008). As they argue, women of colour chick lit subgenres 'tell stories about young women's undivided empowerment, but the characters' engagements with femininity and gender are often articulated through the questions of race, nation, ethnicity and class' (4). Broadly, Heiss's novels are animated by class relations. Her protagonists are depictions of an emergent Aboriginal middle class whose career and dating aspirations are inclusive of the nexus of gender and race. This section redresses some of the limitations identified in contemporary chick lit scholarship before introducing a reader-response based approach as a way of complementing this form of analysis.

Aileen Moreton-Robinson (2000) and Marcia Langton (1993) provide a framework for exploring the intersection of race and gender in the Australian context. In her seminal study, *Talkin'up to the White Woman: Aboriginal Women and Feminism* (2000), Moreton-Robinson unpacks the complicity of Australian feminism in the historical and continuing dispossession of Aboriginal women and people. Central to Australian feminism is the double prong of whiteness and nationality, both of which remain under-theorized and operate as an invisible norm. For Moreton-Robinson, 'whiteness' is both construct and reality: 'whiteness as race, as privilege and as a social construction is not interrogated as a difference within feminist political practice and theory' (xviii). Thus, feminist practice or analysis that does not interrogate this remains arguably complicit in the structures that perpetuate Aboriginal dispossession. The intersectional history of race and gender in Australia is also theorized by Marcia Langton (1993) who argues for the foundational importance of intersectional theoretical approaches to Aboriginal artists: 'without theories of race and gender, which are historically and culturally relevant to Aboriginal people and white Australia, we cannot interpret our artists' (1993: 45). Ideological analysis bolstered by post-feminist critique precludes adequate analysis of these intersectional dimensions and produces readings that focus on the problematics of Heiss's literature.

As noted earlier, paradoxical tyranny and freedom of choice characterize the post-feminist politics of chick lit. An emphasis on career aspiration, dating and conspicuous consumption can, of course, align with explicit racial politics. Perhaps what is most striking about the women of Heiss's literature is their uniform commitment to producing change contingent on operating within existent structures. The protagonists of Heiss's chick lit are embedded in the politics of neo-liberalism, they are explicit consumers and in a sense are the beneficiaries, at least economically, of some existing economic structures. They are, however, interested in social or political

change. For these women, change means challenging negative racial stereotypes or reductive conceptions of Aboriginality through the fields of
education, politics and the arts.

bell hooks's book *Where We Stand: Class Matters* (2000) explores the
intrinsic link between class and race in African American communities. Not
dissimilar to Moreton-Robinson, hooks weaves personal experience with
analysis to unpack how class segregation is built on a history of extended
dispossession of racialized groups. Class analysis, she argues, is often
omitted from discussion of race – but the two are intrinsically tied. In
many respects, Heiss's books are involved in the project of writing race
through the depiction of what has come to be referred to as the 'emergent
Aboriginal middle class' (Langton, 2012). In the article 'Who's afraid of the
black middle class' (2016), Timmah Ball reflects on some of the 'contradictions' of being an Aboriginal middle-class woman. Drawing on the work
of Aboriginal academic Bronwyn Carlsen, Ball notes the widening gap
between Indigenous Australians and how her class position has the dual
effect of invoking feelings of 'shame' and 'anxiety' and also 'erasing
Aboriginality' completely. Ball's internal conflict is partially theorized by
Ludlow et al. (2016), who describe a 'double bind' in which Indigenous
identity that defies racist stereotypes is treated suspiciously, or as 'inauthentic'. As they write, 'the more modern or global Indigeneity is seen as being,
the more its authenticity as an identity is questioned' (2). Drawing on the
work of Gregory Bateson, they further explore the perceived contradictions
and tension of claims to Indigeneity within settler colonial states, 'in which
no matter what a person does, he can't win' (quoted in Ludlow et al.,
2016: 2). The complexity of modern Aboriginal identity is further captured
in the term, 'the soft bigotry of low expectations', a term attributed to
conservative American columnist Michael Gerson, but also theorized by
Marcia Langton and Noel Pearson. This term explains suspicion and
distrust of Indigenous Australians who do not adhere to deficit understanding of Indigeneity, and how this perception is instrumental in keeping
Aboriginal people within a cycle of poverty (Langton, 2012; Pearson, 2016).

The protagonists of Heiss's chick lit have all achieved rapid social
mobility and are identifiable as newly consecrated members of the middle
class. All four woman are university educated: Lauren has a Masters degree

specializing in the appeal of Aboriginal art in an international market (2010: 49), Libby has a degree from the University of Melbourne, and Peta and Alice both received a Bachelor of Education from Sydney's University of Technology. Education provides the mechanism through which the protagonists are elevated to what Langton describes as 'an emergent Aboriginal middle class' (2012), a relatively recent social phenomenon in which Aboriginal Australians have achieved 'radical social uplift through accumulation of social and human capital in the space of one, or no more than three generations (2012). These protagonists have reputable and established careers in the arts, politics and education and hold firm aspirations to further their positions in their respective fields. Alice Aigner (*Not Meeting Mr Right*) is the Head of the History Department at St. Christina's College, a Catholic school. She is the first woman to be appointed to the head of this department (68) and has aspirations to be principal of St. Christina's (79). Lauren (*Manhattan Dreaming*) is an up-and-coming curator at the National Aboriginal Gallery in Canberra who aspires to become its director. Libby (*Paris Dreaming*) also works at the National Aboriginal Gallery as programme manager, but has ambitions to one day become an Ambassador for the Arts. Finally, Peta Tully (*Avoiding Mr Right*) is the National Aboriginal Policy Manager of Media, Sports, Arts, Refugees and Indigenous Affairs with an ambition to eventually become the Minister for Cultural Affairs.

The protagonists' careers are a radical elevation from their respective families' class status. Lauren and Alice are the first of their family to attend university, which is also largely implied for both Peta and Libby. Further, Lauren and Peta both hail from remote country towns and Alice's parents were blue-collar workers. Despite their close connections with their families, the social mobility achieved by this emergent middle class is received suspiciously by both family and friends and colloquially deemed 'Bourgeois Blak' (Heiss, 2011: 43). Heiss caustically critiques broader perceptions of Aboriginal disadvantage. As spoken by Alice in *Avoiding Mr Right*, 'I was a bourgeois black, and so was Peta. It wasn't hard to be in the Aboriginal community – you just had to have a job and own your own car and you were regarded as middle class' (Heiss, 2008: 237). Owing to their accumulated cultural and social capital, some of these women experience a degree of estrangement from their family. Lauren describes herself as a 'boganist' (Heiss, 2010: 81), who is more interested in the 'Big Apple' than the 'Big Banana' or 'Big Avocado' (61). As Langton reminds us in the 2012 *Bower Lecture Series*, 'Counting Our Victories: the End of Garvey-ism and the Soft Bigotry of Low Expectation', however, social mobility does not equate with a capitulation to assimilationist politics. Although Heiss's protagonists all work in government-related industry, these women inhabit positions of authority across a number of fields: the arts, politics and education; and they leverage these positions to influence social and political change.

Each of Heiss's novels is expressly concerned with distinct political debates and concerns framed by distinct societal fields. *Not Meeting Mr Right* positions protagonist Alice within the field of education and features a complication of constructions of Aboriginality and Australian history. *Avoiding Mr Right* takes place within the field of politics and there is a focus on Aboriginal deaths in custody and the institutionalization and exploitation of Aboriginality within academia. *Manhattan Dreaming* and *Paris Dreaming* both take place within the field of cultural production and there is an emphasis on the recognition of Indigenous artists and artwork as deconstructing reductive and stereotypical understandings of Aboriginality.

As mentioned, Alice in *Not Meeting Mr Right* is the first Indigenous and first female Head of the History Department at St. Christina's College. Alice uses her position to correct the way Aboriginal people have been historicized. For example, in discussion of the extension of voting rights to women in Australia, a student points out that this was not the case for Indigenous women. Alice remarks, 'in a class with only one Koori girl, Kerry, it was actually a non-Koori student, Bernardine, who had picked up on this fact. It made me proud' (Heiss, 2007: 67). While Alice's job allows her to instil in her students the significance of challenging or being critical of historical representations of Indigenous Australians, she considers herself to be a 'champagne socialist' (295). In a dating ad she elucidates: 'I like reading historical novels, I literally live at the beach, have done a wine appreciation course and am tertiary educated. I am a champagne socialist with a sense of justice' (295). That is, like the other protagonists of Heiss's literature, Alice is invested in producing change within existing structures.

In *Avoiding Mr Right*, Peta Tully relocates from Sydney to Melbourne to pursue her career aspiration of one day becoming Minister of Cultural Affairs. Her work is inextricably linked with her identity, and her passion for advancing the cause of Indigenous Australians is both personal and career oriented. In conversation with a colleague and frustrated by his ignorance over Indigenous affairs she says: 'The issues I'm talking about are important to me, and not just because of my work. This is who I am. Do you understand that?' (Heiss, 2008: 161). Peta envisages her career as a means of enacting social change. In so doing she eschews the more conventional roles of femininity as care-taker:

> And at the moment I knew that working in policy was what I wanted to be doing with my life. Marriage and kids seriously had to wait. I had a different purpose for the next few years and that was to educate those who worked with Aboriginal people as part of their lives. (192)

In Heiss's literature the visual arts are emphasized as a powerful means of deconstructing and complicating reductive conceptions of Indigeneity as well as celebrating Indigenous culture. Both Libby in *Paris Dreaming* and Lauren in *Manhattan Dreaming* are curators and their engagement in the arts is about celebration and continuance of Indigenous culture and educating non-Indigenous people on Indigenous culture. Describing her presentation on the National Aboriginal Gallery of Victoria to a visiting group of Indigenous curators from Canada, Lauren says 'I was proud to talk about the gallery and the role we played in maintaining Aboriginal culture, and now showcasing it to the world' (Heiss, 2010: 167). Lauren's sentiments encapsulate the politics of Heiss's literature more generally; her work simultaneously both affirms and celebrates Indigenous culture and potentially educates and exposes non-Indigenous peoples to Indigenous culture and affairs. A substantial number of Indigenous artists are mentioned across the two books. Heiss does not mention an artist without qualifying their medium, politics and significance. While visual artists represent the majority of the Indigenous artists mentioned, Heiss also acknowledges the importance of Indigenous musicians, activists and warriors, filmmakers and to a lesser extent, authors. Indigenous artists mentioned in *Manhattan Dreaming* include: Gordon Hookey, Jenny Fraser, Christian Thompson, rea, Adam Hill, Elaine Russell, Julie Dowling, Wayne Quilliam, Karen Mills, Judy Watson, Ricky Maynard, Lin Onus, Destiny Deacon and Darell Sibasado. Each of these artists is discussed in relation to a specific piece of their work. The following artists are mentioned in *Paris Dreaming*: Paddy Nyunkuny Bedford, Tommy Watson, Lena Nyadbi, John Mawurndjul, Gulumbu Yunupingu, Ningura Napurrula, Judy Watson, Michael Riley, Tony Albert, George Nona, Roy Kennedy, Margaret Ross, Emily McDaniel, Michael McDaniel, Vernon Ah Kee, Merril Bray, Zane Saunders and Andrea Fisher. For such short novels this is an impressive number of Indigenous artists, and this does not include further references to specific Indigenous activists, warriors, authors, musicians, film-makers and curators.

Another salient aspect of all these novels is the way they interrogate race relations within Australia and abroad. Heiss foregrounds the politics of race by placing her protagonists in conversation with individuals who represent explicit political positions. This means that Heiss can engage in the complexities of the chosen issue by giving voice to the dissenting side but ultimately revealing the limitations, naivety or ignorance of their positions. Although there are many examples of this technique in her literature, there are two primary characters that exemplify this technique: Simple Simon from *Not Meeting Mr Right*, who believes that Aboriginality is a matter of genetics; and Mike the Cop from *Avoiding Mr Right* who represents a position unsympathetic to the issue of Aboriginal deaths in custody.

These characters represent conservative, naive or racist political positions that are comprehensively addressed and complicated by the respective female protagonists of each novel. In Heiss's literature these characters can represent politics that are capable of reform and address. For example, Mike the Cop remains a central character in *Avoiding Mr Right*, after adopting a more progressive attitude towards deaths in custody in a case related to the 2004 Palm Island death in custody.[7] On his first date with Peta, Mike the Cop wears a charity band in support of the offending officer and argues that

---

[7] In this case a Palm Island resident, Cameron Doomadgee, died in a police cell and his death led to civic disturbances on the island and a legal, political and media

he supports 'due process' (2008: 144). Peta rejects this defence and outlines the injustice of the legal system for Indigenous Australians (145). Subsequently, Mike the Cop, reformed by Peta, removes his support for the offending policeman and ultimately emerges as Peta's love interest for the novel.

Simple Simon is one of the less eligible bachelors featured in *Not Meeting Mr Right*. Simon, it emerges, has recently discovered that he has distant Aboriginal heritage; he has proclaimed his newfound identity and is keen that Alice, as a proud and strong Wiradjuri woman, authenticate and validate his Aboriginality. In her interaction with Simon, Alice communicates the problematics of predicating understandings of Aboriginality based purely on genetic ancestry. Rather forcefully, she confides to the reader, 'Aboriginality is spiritual, and it's a lived experience not something you find by accident and attach its name to yourself. I'm sick of white people deciding they're black so they have some sense of belonging, or worse still, so they can exploit our culture' (2007: 165). These two examples demonstrate how Heiss's literature engages with dominant politics through the prism of individuals.

As encouraged by Butler and Desai (2008), Harzewski (2006) and Farr (2009), this analysis supplants a focus on post-feminist critique for a focus on the intersections of class, race and gender. Heiss's representation of the Aboriginal middle class is a significant form of socio-cultural commentary. Nonetheless, such an approach only partially accounts for the broader social significance of these novels. As pointed out by Farr, there is a compulsion in scholarship on chick lit to focus overwhelmingly on ideological analysis to the detriment of the interpretive possibilities of the field. Farr presents the following solution: analysis based on affect, that is, attention to the way the genre inspires affinity, empathy, affect, entertainment, education and engagement (2009: 209); all qualities excluded from conventional literary analysis. A select number of scholars have begun this work through attention to the experience of the reader (Ramirez, 2009; Mißler, 2016). In the next section I extend this approach through a broadened framework of genre as articulated by John Frow in his book *Genre* (2006).

sensation that continued for three years. Sensationally, the Director of Public Prosecutions acquitted Chris Hurley of Doomadgee's death.

3.5 Genre: a Turn Towards the Reader

Frow's work is significant because it presents genre as neither stable nor singular; it is not a matter of 'taxonomical purity' (2006: 76) and there is no genre 'master list' (2). While I do not seek to advance a new definition of genre in this Element, from this point, I put forward an understanding of genre as a 'framing device', as inspired by Frow's analysis. Frow is less interested in identifying or classifying genre than he is in considering how genre works to produce particular kinds of knowledge and meaning. According to Frow, genre is an organizational practice that contextualizes and delimits the interpretation of a text for the reader. Genre, then, is not a property of the texts itself: 'Genre is neither a property of and located "in" texts, nor a projection of and located "in" readers; it exists as a part of the relationship between texts and readers, and it has a systematic existence' (112). Drawing on Janet Giltrow, Frow further explains how the act of classification simultaneously evokes a discursive community and, thus, genre becomes a question of 'use' (7) that occurs between the textual structure and social situations in which they occur (14).

While scholarship remains largely focussed on the ideological significance of the 'prototypical' chick lit novel, authors of chick lit, such as Cathy Yardley (2006), point out that chick lit 'isn't what they (critics) think it is. It probably isn't even what you think it is. And the parameters and definitions of the genre are changing daily' (4). Contrary to the scholarship on chick lit, Yardley simply defines the genre as, 'the overgeneralized moniker for contemporary women's fiction, with as many facets and faces as contemporary women themselves' (9). Yardley could be quoting Frow himself when she refutes the idea of a genre masterlist: 'a list that is potentially endless, not least because new genres are constantly emerging and old ones changing their function' (Frow, 2006: 30). To return to the point made by Farr, and now supplemented with Frow, analysis of chick lit as a closed-genre convention does indeed appear to be a blunt and restrictive instrument to apply to these novels (Frow, 2006: 110).

Frow's analysis presents the possibility for analysis that is focussed more on the reader than internal analysis of the text. In the case of Heiss's literature, this is arguably productive for a number of reasons. Firstly,

Frow partly presents genre as a means of binding meaning to certain social situations. In Section 1, I discussed how Heiss used the genre to deliver a particular political message. Critical reviews of Heiss's chick lit affirmed the novels as an articulation of the genre, but also noted their explicit political dimension as a point of distinction. Frow emphasizes the subjective and interpretative dimension of genre, and, these elements cannot be measured through internal analysis or even reference to critical reviews. A reader-response approach can also extend and complement the intersectional ideological analysis I have presented on Heiss's novels.

To some extent, this work on reader-response theory and Heiss's novels has been advanced in Mathew's second article, 'Educating the reader in Anita Heiss' chick lit' (2016b). This article is significant in that it seeks to supplant a focus on ideological analysis with a focus on the reader. She presents Heiss's novels as 'advice manuals' that are designed 'to expose readers to the correct norms of behaviours for interacting with Australia's First Peoples' (1). Heiss does also discuss her writing as a pedagogical tool: 'I want them to learn things, but I want all my books to teach in some way' (Heiss, 2017). But, her approach is more evocative of the language of reconciliation with an emphasis on understanding, assistance and discussion than it is bluntly didactic: 'I'm trying to create something that has a lasting life and will be used in classrooms to generate conversations and help people understand their role in society' (Heiss, 2017). Mathew's analysis is premised on a model of education in which Heiss overtly instructs and directs her readership on Indigenous affairs, but this model does not account for the subjective experience of genre articulated by Frow.

3.6 The Cultural Interface: Engagement Not Education

Anne Brewster's scholarship provides a productive way of theorizing a model of reader engagement for Heiss's novels. Her work seeks to understand how protest writing by Aboriginal authors makes race as a social construct apparent to the reader. Although Brewster's theorization often involves a white reader, her thinking is applicable to the broader non-Indigenous community. In particular her work on the protest poetry of Aileen Moreton-Robinson and Lisa Bellear bears relevance for this discussion. Brewster considers how these poets 'engage' (2008: 56), 'position' (2007: 210) and 'interpellate' (2008: 56) the reader. Brewster's articles consider how poems produce a space of encounter between the reader and the Indigenous voice in the text. Brewster also identifies this space as 'a zone of relationality' (2007: 216), 'a zone of interracial sociability' (2008: 56), a space of 'cross racial encounter' (2007: 210) and a 'dialogic, interactive space' (2007: 211). This is achieved through the exposure, or 'witnessing of whiteness' – an idea adapted from Michelle Fine – that makes the reader aware of the salience of race for Australian identity and nationalism (2008: 211).

In her article 'Engaging the public intimacy of whiteness' (2008) Brewster holistically approaches the question of the reading audience. In order to counter a literary tradition that implies a 'disinterested, universal, abstract and disembodied' (56) audience, she proposes the term 'publics', that incorporates the multiple and differentiated audiences drawn to a text (56). She writes:

> I differentiate between the non-Indigenous 'target' group of Indigenous protest (the body of policy-makers that formu-lates governmental management, legislates in Indigenous affairs and produces a discourse of pedagogical nationalism) and 'reference' publics (white liberals who read and disse-minate Indigenous literature). (56)

Through her focus on a reading audience and the Indigenous author, Brewster's scholarship does, to some extent, align with Mathew's. Where she differs is in her disavowal of the idea of education of the reader for a focus on the act of reading as a 'dialogic and interactive space' (2007: 211). With the exception of 'Brokering cross racial feminism', Brewster's work emphasizes that although these texts are not for the white reader, they *can* perform this function. Indigenous authors act as interlocutors: 'addressing, engaging, critiquing and reshaping the knowledge and sensibilities of whiteness and non-Indigenous audiences and publics, thereby reconfiguring cross-cultural relations' (2015: xviii).

Brewster's analysis provides a nuanced means of considering the moment of interaction between text, author and reader. Her work on the 'space' and 'zone' of encounter is significant to this Element and these ideas find greater coherence in her application of Martin Nakata's concept of 'the cultural interface', developed in her book *Giving this Country a Memory* (2015). The cultural interface, in its most distilled form, refers to the space, or zone of negotiation, between traditional Indigenous knowledges and mainstream or Western knowledges (Nakata, 2007: 199). Nakata emphasizes the primacy of Indigenous knowledges and subjectivity as a means of complicating academic discourse and stereotypical understandings of Indigeneity. He writes:

> [The] priority to see the everyday world of the Islander as a productive theoretical space, the Cultural Interface, which is a re-theorisation of the lived position as the space where generations of Islander people make and remake themselves as they encounter competing and changing traditions. (12)

To adapt this for the act of reading we can theorize the cultural interface as the moment in which views about Indigenous people are met with representation by Indigenous people; that is, the moment in which Indigeneity is no longer objectified and is instead reaffirmed by Indigenous subjectivity and experience.

To summarize, scholarship that presupposes a 'normative', 'traditional' or 'prototypical' expression of chick lit as a genre lends itself to the logic that supposed incarnations of the genre by women of colour are deviant. This tradition is aided by the propensity to legitimate and evaluate the value of the genre with respect to second-wave feminism, an approach that occludes the histories of women of colour. Although my ideological reading of Heiss's novels seeks to redress this, this form of analysis still only goes some way towards accounting for the broader significance of these novels. Mathew's consideration of the reader is a productive development in extending the boundaries of scholarship in the field. Her analysis, however, reduces the complexity of the reading act by proposing a hypodermic model of education. Again, this conclusion is drawn from a singularly ideological reading of the novels.

The next section departs from an ideological reading of the novels, and draws on Frow's more porous understanding of genre to incorporate readers' perspectives on Heiss's chick lit. This is undertaken through analysis of reviews and surveys collected from reviewers on the book-reviewing website Goodreads.

4 The Reader: Goodreads Reviews of Heiss's Chick Lit

As demonstrated in Sections 1 and 2, critics and scholars are divided over the extent to which the political dimension of Heiss's chick lit is reconcilable with the focus on fun and consumerism definitive of the genre (Becerra-Gurley, 2007; Guivarra, 2007; Fullerton, 2010; Kaye, 2011; Ommundsen, 2011; Mathew, 2016a). Drawing on reader responses collected from Goodreads, I am interested in how readers perceive the argued disjuncture delineated between politics and genre identified in Heiss's chick lit. More generally, this discussion also interrogates a perception that chick lit resists the expression of politics of racial and ethnic difference (Oggunaike, 2004; Ferriss and Young, 2006; Morrison, 2010; Ommundsen, 2011; Mathew, 2016a). As of 3 September 2018 Goodreads features over 80-million reviews with membership numbering in excess of 80-million (Goodreads, n.d.). Cecilia Konchar Farr (2009) suggests that scholars of chick lit supplant an ideological or cultural approach with a focus on affect; that is, attention to the way the genre inspires affinity, empathy, affect, entertainment, education and engagement. Goodreads reviews provide an ideal opportunity to pursue this analysis as reviews are emotional and observably self-reflexive (Rehberg Sedo, 2003; Steiner, 2008). Ultimately, reader-generated reviews are a valuable source for researchers interested in exploring the cogency of genre as an interpretive frame and for testing scholastic arguments pertaining to the boundaries of genre in chick lit.

In the first half of this section, I draw on discussion of different formations of group-based reading communities including book clubs, mass reading events and online reading communities. I argue that across reading-studies scholarship there exist recurrent themes and ideas irrespective of the articulation of the formation of the reading group.[8] I put forward the term 'Social Reading Formations' (SRFs) to capture the various articulations of reading groups that are composed of a dialogic and interactive component

---

[8] Different formations of reading groups include: literary salons; author–reader relationships; face-to-face book clubs; television programmes; online chat rooms; formal reading groups designed by cultural authorities; and mass reading events.

formed around a text.[9] While critics such as Anna S. Ivy argue that it is naive to generalize about reading groups, as they take many forms and serve many purposes (quoted in Rehberg Sedo, 2011: 11), I suggest that attention to these recurrent themes and ideas can be beneficial in the analysis of new social valences of reading, such as online reading platforms. Within this context, I consider reader reviews of Heiss's four chick lit novels: *Not Meeting Mr Right*, *Avoiding Mr Right*, *Manhattan Dreaming* and *Paris Dreaming*. In the second half of this section I expand on this discussion through analysis of responses to a survey that I conducted with Goodreads reviewers. These responses provide the opportunity to extend the question of genre and definition as well as the idea of personal transformation and education of the reader.

This section argues that, despite its marketing, chick lit may not be the singular frame through which Heiss's chick lit is read. Readers' interpretations of Heiss's literature are not only delineated by genre, but also informed by her authorial presence, and the political dimensions of the novels. Readers' appraisal of Heiss's novels depends less on a formulaic understanding of genre than on quality of writing, characterization and storytelling. Not only do these findings point to the individual and subjective nature of the reading experience, but also complicate academic understandings of Heiss's literature that perceive the political dimension of her novels to be in tension with the genre components of chick lit.

Ultimately, these findings suggest potential new directions for chick lit scholarship, as a reader-based approach demonstrates the readers' understanding of genre as more porous than that previously expressed in chick lit scholarship.

4.1 Goodreads and Social Reading Formations

Goodreads was founded in December 2006 and publicly launched in January 2007 with a membership that numbered around 650,000 (Goodreads,

---

[9] In this section I define the responses collected from Goodreads as reviews and not commentary. Although online reviews are arguably based in the language of emotion, a metric of criticism distinct from academic reviewing practices, responses still operate as a form of recommendation based on a star classification system and critical analysis of the text.

n.d.) and a catalogue of approximately 10 million books. As of 3 September 2018 Goodreads features over 80 million reviews and members, with 2.3 billion catalogued books (Goodreads, n.d.). Goodreads's guiding mission is to 'help people find and share the books they love'. The website is comprised of three core features: book discovery; content access; and user interaction. In simple terms Goodreads identifies itself as a site for readers and for book recommendations. Scholars, however, differ in their classification of the site. Primarily, minor distinctions occur around the degree to which the site can be characterized as a social media platform. In scholarship, Goodreads has been classified as a 'bibliocentric networking site' (Foasberg, 2012; Naik, 2012), a 'social media platform' (Vlieghe, Muls and Rutten, 2016) and as a 'hybrid site' that is neither entirely a book-based or social network site (Thelwall and Kousha, 2017). Lisa Nakamura (2013) stresses hybridity by defining Goodreads as a 'biblio-centric' and 'egocentric' network of public reading performance (240). Mike Thelwall and Kayvan Kousha (2017) provide a comprehensive overview of the presumed identity of the Goodreads reader to conclude that the site is composed of predominantly female users. Based on analysis of over 50,000 Goodreads accounts, they conclude that approximately 75 per cent of the site's users are female. This statistic largely coheres with current estimates that women readers constitute roughly 80 per cent of the fiction market and also extends a tradition that identifies reading groups as historically female spaces (1).

Online SRFs are a relatively recent social phenomenon. Their appearance, however, is not without precedent. As argued by DeNel Rehberg Sedo (2003), 'on-line [reading groups] have roots in off-line realities' (86). Drawing on Elizabeth Long's ethnographic study of reading groups, *Book Clubs: Women and the Uses of Reading and Everyday Life* (2003), Rehberg Sedo (2003) and Ann Steiner (2008) link online reading groups to their face-to-face counterparts. These scholars extend Long's study and argue that through dialogue – and literature's inherent capacity to foster personal identification – women's reading groups can become sites of social change. That is, they can be personally transformative and democratic spaces. As argued by Rehberg Sedo (2011), 'shared reading is both a social process and social formation' (1). Rehberg Sedo (2003, 2011) and Nancy Foasberg (2012) emphasize that these transformative and democratic elements are arguably consistent with online SRFs. Drawing on her edited collection, *Reading Communities from Salons to Cyberspace* (2011), Rehberg Sedo identifies two linking phenomena in historical and contemporary SRFs. The first is the notion of 'community'; the second is the role of 'education' (2). Foasberg echoes this characterization by emphasizing the centrality of the idea of community in SRFs and identifying their 'educational potential' (2012: 50). SRFs are social formations that afford discussion and debate. In particular, this idea of connection and exchange is intimately linked to the argument for the transformative potential of reading groups located in what Rehberg Sedo describes as 'organic dialogic democracy' (2003: 85). For both Rehberg Sedo and Foasberg (2012), the act of reading within a social framework is a community-building exercise (5). That is, reading can be considered to be a social act with public ramifications. This argument is extended in Fuller and Rehberg Sedo's study *Reading Beyond the Book: the Social Practices of Contemporary Literary Culture* (2013). In this study they extend Lauren Berlant's (1997) concept of 'the intimate public sphere' (viii) to mass reading event, in order to theorize the 'citizen reader' (viiii) who, very simplistically, participates in a community that is unified by consumer culture. They write, '[the reader] participates in a public that is produced by the consumption of "common texts and things," which appear to articulate a shared emotional knowledge, and thus proffer the fantasy of "emotional contact" with others' (2013: viiii).

The nature of online reading, interpretation and discussion reflects that of face-to-face SRFs. Ann Steiner (2008) defines online reviewing practices as 'private criticism'; she is quick to note, however, that this is not a new social phenomenon, but does remain historically distinct in its online expression. Private criticism differs from 'established criticism' – a form of critique associated with academic institutions and literary reviewers – with respect to its heightened emotional quality, tone and self-identificatory practices. Rehberg Sedo (2003) further argues that discussion occurs around emotional bonds and, 'promotes an avenue for women to try on new ideas, to share experiences' (85). Online reading and reviewing is, thus, arguably emotional and observably self-reflexive. This form of criticism dually provides an alternative to the restrictive language of aesthetic literary criticism and an opportunity to explore the subjective experience of the embodied, not the implied, reader.

Goodreads, and other online SRFs, have also been argued to be spaces that are especially accommodating for readers of genre fiction. Goodreads has been described as a community of fans who are comparable to readers of popular fiction conceptualized in critical genre theory. Driscoll (2016) extends the idea of 'textual productivity' distinctive of fan studies to include online SRFs Amazon and Goodreads. She argues that 'a reader who creates a textual response to a book, author or a genre is a fan' (425). This is not to say that all online reviewers are necessarily fans, but that the format is conducive to fan culture in its support of textual productivity. Nakamura (2013) identifies Goodreads as both 'a literary network and fan community' (240). Although Nakamura does not qualify her use of this term, we can consider this idea in relation to Gelder's (2004) theorization of popular-fiction readers as distinctly 'loyal' (81). Gelder acknowledges the presence of fans in the field of popular fiction (81). He notes that their engagements can be 'intellectual and even quasi-academic' (75) and that their competence in genre convention makes them 'careful discriminators of the field' (36). Textual responses generated on online SRFs, therefore, are valuable sources for research on questions of definition and qualitative judgement of genre fiction.

4.1.1 Aims and Significance

Reading-studies scholarship conducted on chick lit has generally focussed on the question of genre innovation (Mathew, 2016a; Butler and Desai, 2008) and, in conjunction with the designation of chick lit as *not serious* literature, how online reader criticism of chick lit challenges the broader metrics of literary criticism (Steiner, 2008). Mißler's study is a unique departure in approach, as she attends to the question of how readers make sense of their chosen genre (2016: 3). For Heiss, only Mathew has considered a reading-studies approach in which she argues that her literature operates as an advice manual and analyses its 'pedagogical function' for the reader (2016b: 5). Despite the limited scholarship in this area, an early article in chick lit scholarship bears direct relevance for the analysis undertaken in this section. In 'Manolos, marriage, and mantras: chick-lit criticism and transnational feminism' (2008) Butler and Desai consider the disjuncture between politics and genre in their analysis of South Asian American chick lit. Unlike much scholarship on chick lit that privileges an ideological reading of the genre, their analysis is significant in that they integrate reader responses in the form of online reviews. Drawing on online reviews of the novel *Goddess for Hire*, Butler and Desai argue that responses are polarized. Reviewers identify the novel as either: 'a well written addition to the genre with a South Asian twist' or, 'a mediocre example of formulaic chick lit devoid of any real creativity' (26). Butler and Desai's study is significant in establishing a precedent for analysis of this interpretative disjuncture. However, their analysis of reader reviews is only perfunctory – about one paragraph – and operates only to affirm the extent to which the novel may be read as a successful representation of the genre.

I am interested in a more sustained and nuanced exploration of this argued disjuncture by attending to the subjective nature of reading through an understanding of genre as a framing device and supplemented by Hans Robert Jauss's work on 'the horizon of expectations' (1970). According to Frow (2006), genre is an organizational practice that contextualizes and delimits the interpretation of a text for the reader. It is, however, only a 'fuzzy' organizational practice (80). Jauss's work on the horizon of expectations (1970) is also important in establishing a more flexible frame for interpreting reader reviews of Heiss' chick lit. Jauss puts forward the idea of the horizon of expectations as a structure that informs how a reader interprets and appraises a text. Jauss's theory considers how interpretations diverge based on the historical and cultural moment; an idea not dissimilar to Frow's understanding of genre as an organizational practice that contextualizes and delimits the interpretation of a text for the reader.

For Heiss this is particularly significant. She is neither clearly aligned with the heteronomous or autonomous poles of the literary field. Her writing appeals to a broad and differentiated reading public as she fuses the logics and practices of popular fiction with the ideas and concerns of her academic work. A focus on readers' expectations of the texts allows for a more nuanced analysis of the disjuncture between politics and genre expressed in Heiss's literature. Drawing on Frow and Jauss, this next section considers the expectations that readers bring to bear on Heiss's literature; whether readers delineate the binary of politics versus genre raised by scholars in the field, or whether these reviews demonstrate distinct understandings of the novels outside of the frame of chick lit.

4.1.2 Methodology

A thematic review of reader responses demonstrates that, despite its marketing, chick lit may not be the singular frame through which Heiss's chick lit is read. My analysis of reviews collected from Goodreads ultimately revealed that readers approach Heiss's chick lit from three possible points of departure: as chick lit; as Aboriginal literature defined by the 'nexus of the political and the literary' (Heiss and Minter, 2014: 3); and as both.

I collected sixty-five qualitative reviews from Goodreads, that is, all the reviews that included a written response. I have omitted star-based responses from my analysis. Although these solely star-based responses demonstrate components of the review in that they act as a classification system of merit, they omit the critical rationale outlining their classification and are accordingly of less utility in this study. In total there were twenty-four written responses on *Not Meeting Mr Right*, sixteen on *Avoiding Mr Right*, twenty on *Manhattan Dreaming* and five on *Paris Dreaming* in June 2016. I have discussed the novels as a consistent group owing to their shared universe, in which related characters experience a similar story of personal development. To interpret my raw data, I employed a basic grounded-theory approach. There are divergent understandings of this theory, therefore, my approach is informed by the broad definition put forward by Kathy Charmaz and Atony Bryant in *The Sage Encyclopedia of Qualitative Research Methods* (2008): 'a set of systematic, but flexible, guidelines for conducting inductive qualitative inquiry aimed toward theory construction.' My process involved: coding the data in a rudimentary fashion to look for emergent themes or ideas followed by the definition and sorting of this data into established categories.

As a way of identifying reviewers' expectations of the novels I returned to Gelder's (2004) work on genre. According to Gelder all reading of popular fiction is 'leisured' (23) and read for 'entertainment' (35), and the genre of romance, in particular, is understood as an act of escape (51). As introduced at the beginning of this Element, Ann Steiner (2008) provides a cogent summary of reader expectations and reader experience of chick lit that is not dissimilar to Gelder's more general theorization of popular fiction: 'Good chick lit novels are defined as fun, witty, easy and light reads dealing with real issues. Readers have to be able to sympathise with the main character; identification is, of course, the foundation of the genre' (sec. 5.14).

In Steiner's consideration of Amazon reviews of the chick lit novel *The Wonder Spot*, she reinforces Gelder's understanding of genre readers as highly knowledgeable and 'quasi academic' (75) and argues that readers of chick lit display 'meta-literary' competence and are highly adept at identifying genre and defining its boundaries. Steiner's definition of chick lit, supplemented by Gelder's more general theorization of popular fiction, provides a strong framework against which to interpret reader reviews in that the language that reviewers use to review a text demonstrates the expectations and, accordingly, the interpretative frame that they have brought to the text.

Through a preliminary overview of the reviews on Goodreads for Heiss's four novels: *Not Meeting Mr Right*, *Avoiding Mr Right*, *Manhattan Dreaming* and *Paris Dreaming* the following themes emerged:

- Comedy (funny or not funny)
- Feminist credentials of the text (sexist, not feminist or empowering)
- Education (providing or not providing new perspectives on Aboriginality for the reader)
- Characterization (likeability and relatability of the protagonist)
- Mention of places (Melbourne, Sydney, New York, Paris, Canberra)
- Mention of Aboriginal voice and perspective
- Mention of politics (too polemic or expository)
- Quality of writing (easy to read or badly written)
- Meta-literary competence ('so chick litty', or a 'good' or 'bad' take on chick lit)
- Mention of the author and her profession.

Following this, I coded these reviews based on whether they reflected aspects of the definition of chick lit outlined above. In order to refine my data I decided that reviews must exhibit at least two of the criteria put forward by Steiner and supplemented by Gelder to be classified as related to chick lit.

Generally, the list above corresponded to criteria that Steiner defines as constitutive of chick lit. Already, readers seemed to be demonstrating their competence in chick lit by making distinctions about the extent to which the text fulfilled genre criteria based on the novel's comedic qualities and the protagonists' characterizations. Reviews were coded as interpreting the novels through the frame of chick lit based on whether they mentioned the genre explicitly or used the language of 'fun, witty, light read; escape and leisure'. Thirty-five out of sixty-five reviewers identified the novel in accordance with this interpretative frame of chick lit. A thematic review of reader responses demonstrates that, despite its marketing, chick lit may not be the singular frame through which Heiss's chick lit is read. The remaining thirty reviews were not necessarily classifiable according to the language of chick lit. These reviews, instead, include themes such as 'new perspectives', 'polemicism', 'Aboriginality' and 'focus on place'.

In this next section I further refine and outline these remaining thirty reviews to isolate and explore other distinct interpretative lenses that exist outside of the language of chick lit. This includes: 'short reviews'; reviews that focus on place; miscellaneous reviews; and, finally, reviews that use the language of politics. I classified sixteen of the sixty-five reviews as what I term 'short reviews', a practice that reacts primarily on overall impression. They are not substantially self-reflexive and instead are largely emotional in response. Emotion at the expense of considered critical reflection means that short reviews are very brief; sometimes only one sentence long. For example, one reviewer wrote of *Avoiding Mr Right*: 'Blugh! Awful, awful, awful'. Another on *Not Meeting Mr Right*: 'waste of time'. Although short reviews display little critical self-reflexivity, they remain significant and warrant mention in this study as a perfunctory response is just as significant as an elaborate one. Nonetheless, because they lack self-reflexivity, they do not provide adequate information to make an assessment that goes beyond ascribing whether the reader views the books negatively or positively; there is not enough information to enquire into the reader's expectations of the text. For this reason, I do not attend to this class of review further.

A small portion of reviews, three in total, focussed only on place. Australia features prominently in all novels, specifically Canberra, Sydney and Melbourne locations. One reviewer commented that reading *Manhattan Dreaming*, 'made me think nostalgically about things from Australia', suggesting that they are reading from abroad. Another wrote that they 'love reading about places [they] LOVE', in this case Canberra. A further three remaining responses were categorized as 'miscellaneous'. These responses referred to reviewers' personal websites or were in a foreign language.

More numerous and substantial, however, were reviews that focussed on the politics of the text; those that explicitly reference Aboriginal affairs and the racial politics of the novel. Along with reviews that used the language of chick lit, reviews that employed the language of politics constituted the third most substantive interpretative lens after short reviews. Often, these discussions also feature an explicit mention of the author. Of the fifteen responses that discuss the politics of the text eight also reference the author. Significantly, seven of the reviews that used the language of politics also employed the identifying language of chick lit. Although, there remains a discernible divide between readers who approach the texts through the interpretative lens of chick lit and those who interpret the novel outside of the language of genre; the reviewers that employ the dual language of politics and chick lit, seven in total, demonstrate that the interpretative lens readers bring to bear on Heiss's literature is complex, and eludes a simplistic categorization of her literary output.[10]

In the next section I further interrogate these findings by considering how readers' expectations of the text as delineated by either chick lit or through a politically inflected frame influences the overall reading experience, enjoyment and appraisal of the novel. This allows for a consideration of the extent to which classification of genre may affect qualitative readings of the text. In order to qualify whether reviewers' expectations were met or evaded by the novels, I attended to the qualifying language used in the reviews. Figure 1 presents a breakdown of thematic reviews.

4.2 Reader Expectations: the Language of Chick Lit

In discussing genre, readers have already delineated their expectations of the chick lit novel; that it is fun and witty, with identifiable and likeable characters. Overall, thirty-five reviewers identified Heiss's novels as chick lit, fifteen of whom explicitly used the term 'chick lit' in their response and another two using the term 'Aboriginal chick lit'.

---

[10] To clarify: twenty-eight reviews just discussed the novels through the interpretative frame of chick lit; <u>eight</u> reviews discussed the novels using the language of politics; and <u>seven</u> discussed the novels using both.

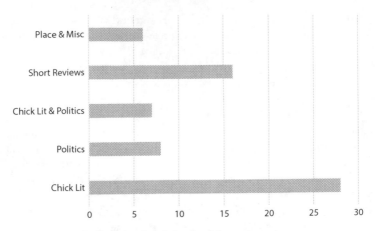

Figure 1 Graph depicting breakdown of thematic reviews

In order to ascertain whether reviewers' expectations were met or not met by the novels I considered the qualitative language used in the reviews; that is, whether the identifying language of genre outlined by Steiner was discussed in positive or negative terms. I classified a reviewer as having had their expectations of the novel met if they discussed at least two elements of the genre in a positive way. For example, 'the novel *is* funny and easy to read'. For a review to be classified as not having its expectations met, the reviewer had to discuss two identifying elements of the genre in a negative way, for example, 'the novel is *not* funny and *not* easy to read'. Reviewers who only had their expectations partly met were those who discussed the novels in equally positive and negative ways. Of the reviews that I identified as using the language of chick lit twelve used language suggesting that their expectations of the novels were *not* met, four used language indicating that their expectations were partly met and nineteen used language indicating that their expectations *were* met. At times, reviewers present similar language in their assessment of the novels, but diverge on whether their expectations of the novel were met. For example, one reviewer who read *Not Meeting Mr Right* disliked the aspects of the novel that, according to Steiner's definition, make it a 'good' example of chick lit (Steiner, 2008: sec.

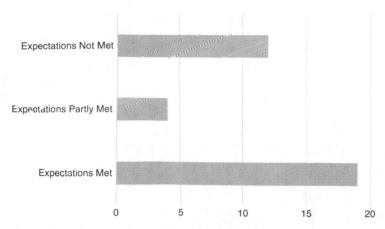

Figure 2 Graph depicting breakdown of expectations of reviewers who use the language of chick lit

5.14). They wrote: 'Easy to read, easy to digest, easy to finish ... and remember not much of it. Lose yourself for a couple of hours stuff, but leaves you hungry for a book that makes you think.' Conversely, another reviewer who read *Paris Dreaming* uses similar language to discuss how their expectations of the novel were met: 'Enjoyable. Followed the usual tropes of romance but was much more intelligent and engaged, in a light-hearted, light-handed way with political issues.' This kind of divergence underscores that interpretation of genre can be individual and subjective. Figure 2 presents a breakdown of the expectations of reviewers who use the language of chick lit.

As defined by Steiner, identification with the main character is the 'foundation' of chick lit (Steiner, 2008: sec. 5.14). The reviewers whom I have coded as having their expectations met reference characterization and discuss the protagonists of Heiss's novels in positive terms. Lauren from *Manhattan Dreaming* is discussed as 'amazing', while another reviewer emphasizes the quality of her characterization: 'loved this story I could imagine the characters – actually I think I know these people!' Two reviewers discuss the protagonist Peta from *Avoiding Mr*

Right. One wrote that '[she's] an amazing character . . . confident, funny and up for a good time', the other comments that she was initially frustrated by the character but grew to like her. A further reviewer personally identifies with Lauren from *Manhattan Dreaming*, in that, as an Indigenous woman the character explicitly challenges racial stereotypes. She writes:

> Often Indigenous peoples consciously change or moderate
> their behaviour to accommodate others and to consciously
> attempt to break down some of the stereotypes, (ie. Lauren's
> being on time or early for everything in an attempt to break
> the stereotype of 'Koori time'. I giggled out loud at this one,
> as it is something I consistently do for those very reasons).

Of the reviewers who demonstrate expectations as being partially met, two discuss the protagonists of *Manhattan Dreaming* and *Paris Dreaming*, the latter writing that 'she found the main character a bit mean so [she] didn't warm to her'. Six of the twelve reviewers whose expectations were *not* met negatively discuss characterization. Primarily, this corresponded to the 'unlikeability' of the main characters. Reviewers found the protagonists of *Avoiding Mr Right* and *Not Meeting Mr Right* respectively 'unlikeable' and 'alienating'.

A number of reviewers expressed disappointment with the quality of the writing. A reviewer who read *Not Meeting Mr Right* wrote: 'A great idea but poorly written.' Another wrote of *Avoiding Mr Right*, 'possibly one of the worst chick lit books I've ever read. Awful characters, stilted dialogue and terrible plot. Arrggh, just a painful read.' These reviews deepen an understanding that reader expectations and enjoyment is predicated on the quality of the literature rather than simply its adherence to formula.

Other reviewers indicated that their expectations of the novels were eluded in a positive way. In their analysis of reader responses focussed on the Richard and Judy Book Club, Fuller and Rehberg Sedo (2013) observe a phenomenon that they term the 'dance of distinction', which signals 'readers' resistance towards popular forms of book culture as they work to maintain their own distinctiveness through articulation of taste' (83). Six of the reviewers preface their responses with their aversion to the genre. This included the responses: 'I hardly ever read so called *chick lit*' and, 'first thing's first, chick lit isn't really my thing'. These reviewers demonstrate surprise regarding their enjoyment of these novels. Reasons for enjoyment differ from reader to reader. One writes that 'there is a much deeper dialogue taking place', another wrote that she read an interview with Heiss and she, 'didn't sound like she was going to write the normal crap'. This reviewer clearly indicates that she 'can't stand the pretentious wank, the incredibly stupid and unlikable heroines and even more stupid storylines', that is, Heiss's literature is an exception to this reviewer's usual reading tastes. Generally, these reviewers indicate how the novels challenged and exceeded the negative conceptions they hold of the genre. Still, they classify these books categorically as chick lit, thus challenging the argument that these books deviate from genre.

4.3 Reader Expectations: the Language of Politics

Reader responses that use the discernible language of chick lit express a readily identifiable framework against which their expectations can be read. Reviewers who read the novels in accordance with this definition overwhelmingly indicated that their expectations had been met. Responses that discuss the texts in accordance with a consideration of the politics of the novels are more resistant to a clearly discernible consideration of expectations. Seven of these reviews are cross-coded with reviews pertaining to chick lit; however, they also demonstrate sustained or explicit consideration of the politics of these novels. As noted, the explicit nature of these reviews provides some insight into the readers' expectations of the novels. These reviews demonstrate four evident themes: firstly, a sense that the novels are didactic; secondly, the extent to which the novels provide new perspectives on Aboriginality; thirdly, that the novels balance politics with genre convention; and finally, the significance of the author in providing the impetus for reading her books.

Reviewers who express criticism of Heiss's literature emphasize the 'antagonistic', 'didactic', 'alienating' and 'heavy handed' presentation of politics in her literature. Frustration or rejection of the politics in Heiss's literature is perhaps indicative of, in Jauss's terms, the evasion of the readers' horizon of expectations. The diversity of these reviews, however, is reflective of Heiss's ambition to 'reach an audience of non-Aboriginal women – largely aged between 18 and 45 years of age – who may not have cared about Aboriginal women in Australia before' (Heiss, 2012: 215). One reviewer discusses Heiss's politics as 'hypocritical' and another qualifies *Not Meeting Mr Right* as 'terrible'. Two reviewers demonstrate that their politics largely cohere with Heiss; however, they reject the presentation of these politics as articulated by the main protagonist. These reviewers do not reject the politics of the novels; just the way that those politics are presented. As identified by Mathew, the distinct passages that represent a switch to exposition are didactic in tone (2016a: 5). As one reviewer put it, '[*Manhattan Dreaming*] is all telling and no showing' and the novel is 'didactic (read: condescending).' Another reviewer indicates that despite being a white ally of Indigenous affairs, 'A black-arm banded whitefella multiculturalist female academic', with clear sympathies for the protagonist's political and historical views, the expression and presentation of this 'clear political agenda' in *Not Meeting Mr Right* is 'antagonistic and alienating'. Significantly, this reviewer discusses her criticism of the text within the politics of reconciliation. Her primary criticism is that the novel '[precludes] all possibility of a reconciliatory conversation'. Implicit in this criticism is an expectation of the text – the promotion and expression of politics as 'reconciliatory'.

In a similar vein, reviewers also comment on the extent to which the novels provide new perspectives on Aboriginality. For example, one reviewer expresses disappointment with *Not Meeting Mr Right*: 'it was absolutely disappointing in respect to the Aboriginal culture. I'm not Aboriginal but I didn't really get any idea of what it is like from the story.' This reviewer demonstrates an expectation of 'new perspectives', that is, a desire for education. This expectation is unmet as they conclude that '[they] stepped away from the book not learning anything new'. These two readers demonstrate divergent expectations of the texts through the frame of Aboriginal literature rather than genre. These reviews again demonstrate that while Aboriginal literature and the nature of online SRFs may be conducive to the possibility of personal transformation and education, this is highly contingent on the reader and the expectations that they bring to bear on the text. As argued by Mathew (2016c) in her article 'Reviewing race in the digital literary sphere', online SRFs provide a unique space to examine readers' negotiation of racial identity. As much as literature *can* perform the function of producing transformation and the fostering of anti-racist coalitions, scholarship has yet to adequately engage with the possibility that literature, especially when mediated through online SRFs, may further compound racial stereotypes; primarily, because the nature of this scholarship has focused exclusively on face-to-face SRFs.

Other reviewers, however, did enjoy the political dimensions of the novels. One wrote that 'the them and us was a little heavy' but still found this 'refreshing'. Another, emphatically characterized the diversity of representation in *Manhattan Dreaming* as 'fabulous'. This reviewer is excited by the relative absence of 'white characters' from the novel. They wrote:

> Basically, the only white character of any significance is Lauren's douchebag boyfriend, Adam, who's a rugby player. So from a diversity perspective seeing true-to-life Indigenous characters from a range of communities around the world? YES. 10/10 would recommend.

Five reviewers indicated that the political dimension of the novels worked well with the conventions of the genre. Seven reviews in total used the identifying language of chick lit and politics. One reviewer discussed her pleasure at the representation of diversity in *Manhattan Dreaming*: 'The diversity in this book is FABULOUS. I mean, how often do you see diverse characters in a leading role in chick lit? Almost never, in my experience.' Another reviewer wrote of *Paris Dreaming*: 'Enjoyable. Followed the usual tropes of romance but was much more intelligent and engaged, in a light-hearted, light- handed way with political issues.' That is, reviewers who approached Heiss's novels through the dual frame of genre and politics overwhelmingly had their expectations met. Thereby challenging the perception that the political dimension of these novels is irreconcilable with the genre (Becerra-Gurley, 2007; Guivarra, 2007; Fullerton, 2010; Kaye, 2011; Ommundsen, 2011; Mathew, 2016a).

As discussed in Section 1, Heiss's work as an academic also plays a significant role in her identity as an author. Lahire's conception of the second job helps us understand Heiss's work in academia as entirely complementary and constitutive of her overall public profile. While scholarship on genre acknowledges that the industry of popular fiction is partially defined by the public role of the author, who is intimately connected to their readership through quick turnaround of output, Heiss remains unusual in that her role as an academic and activist further characterizes her role as an author. Accordingly, some reviewers identified Heiss's second job as what attracted them to her literature and characterized their enjoyment based on how this translates into the novels. Two reviewers demonstrated how the author prompted them to put aside their prejudices about the genre. Both reviewers were 'intrigued' by the author, respectively, having read an interview with her and seeing her in a talk. They both characterize her as 'interesting' and as a 'fun intelligent person'. One reviewer reflects that the novel *Not Meeting Mr Right* was not the 'normal crap' while the other dismisses the book *Manhattan Dreaming* as instantly 'boring' and reflects that, 'I should have trusted my gut in judging books by their cover. I'd never have given this book a second glance by cover alone'. In these instances the self-presentation of the author is enough to compel and alter readers' prejudices regarding genre.

4.4 Surveys Collected from Goodreads Reviewers

In the previous section I applied the work of Frow and Jauss as a way of understanding the interpretative frame that readers bring to bear on Heiss's chick lit and how these expectations affect the qualitative reading experience. Overwhelmingly, reviewers approached Heiss's literature through the interpretative frame of chick lit and indicated that their expectations *were* met. Even reviewers who employed the dual language of chick lit and politics produced a similar outcome. In this section, I extend this discussion through analysis of responses to a survey that I conducted with Goodreads reviewers. These responses provide the opportunity to substantially extend two ideas raised in the previous section. First, the question of genre and definition, not through the framework of expectation, but through analysis of what I term 'route-to-reader'; that is, *why* a reviewer chose to read these books. Second, this section interrogates the idea of personal transformation and education of the reader; ideas particular to SRFs as well as scholarship on Heiss's novels. This is undertaken through a return to Brewster's application of Nakata's concept of the cultural interface.

4.4.1 Methodology

Between December 2016 and March 2017 I collected thirty-four survey responses from Goodreads users who had reviewed Heiss's chick lit novels. Surveys were sent out to all sixty-five reviewers analysed in the previous section. The survey consisted of nine questions that were generally designed to construct a clearer profile of reviewers' reading tastes, preferences and personal identity; and to measure the reviewers' enjoyment of the novels and the degree to which they found Heiss's novels to be educational. The specific wording of this final question, and its focus on education, was influenced by a number of distinct factors. This included Mathew's understanding of Heiss's literature as 'advice manuals' that educate the reader (2016b), Heiss's desire that her novels educate: 'I want all my books to teach in some way, I don't want to waste trees' (Heiss, 2017), critical reviews that show the significance of the novels as educative for a non-Indigenous audience (Guivarra, 2007) and scholarship that emphasizes the transformative dimensions of SRFs.

4.4.2 Analysis of Route-to-Reader

The survey allowed respondents to qualify *why* they chose to read Heiss's chick lit novels, thereby providing potential further insight into the impact of Heiss's multiple authorial personas in attracting a diverse reading audience. The reasons why and how audiences take up Heiss's literature is referred to as the 'route-to-reader'. In keeping with the previous analysis of Goodreads reviews, there is a demarcation between those who use the language of genre, and those who use the language of politics in their explanation of why they chose to read the novels. Given the understanding that genre establishes the frame of interpretation and expectations that readers bring to bear on a text, analysis of route-to-reader provides further insight into the conditions that produce this interpretative frame. The route-to-reader pathway for Heiss's chick lit can be summarized in the following ways: through the novels' paratextual elements; through recommendation by an individual or institution; through exposure to the author; through a conscious desire to locate literature by women of colour; and thorough serendipitous events.

A number of respondents suggest that they were influenced by the novels' para- textual elements, specifically the book design. To return to Heiss's discussion with her publisher: 'the women who buy these books know what they are looking for, they'll go in the shop and they don't know specifically the title of the author [but] they will look for a book that looks like the one they just read' (Heiss, 2017). One respondent made the decision to read *Not Meeting Mr Right* based on perfunctory analysis of the paratextual elements of the novel: 'It caught my attention, as it was something different to what I usually see. From the blurb, the novel sounded like a fun and easy read.' Another also uses the language of sight to explain route-to-reader: '*Avoiding Mr Right* caught my eye when it was just what I needed.' A further respondent continues this theme: 'I picked it up thinking it was a romance, and I was interested to see the representation of Indigenous Australian characters in this genre.'

Another discernible theme in analysis of the route-to-reader is the role of individuals and institutions in recommending literature to the respondent. One respondent based her decision to read Heiss's literature on recommendation from her library: 'they were available via my library as an e-book and probably were on the recommended page (or maybe just under the romance category and I've read almost all of my libraries [*sic*] romance novels).' Another respondent who read *Paris Dreaming* wrote, 'My mum had it on her bookshelf'. Another dominant route-to-reader pathway is that which is mediated by authorial participation in different events and digital platforms. This includes social media, podcasts, radio interviews, writers' festivals and newspaper articles. Overall, seven respondents chose to read Heiss's chick lit based on Heiss's media presence, and a further two were led to her chick lit after reading her memoir.

The remaining respondents were drawn to read Heiss's chick lit based on a desire for new perspectives on Aboriginality. These reviewers are drawn to the political content of Heiss's work and are engaged in the effort to read literature by women of colour to correct a monocultural reading history. One writes that they read Heiss's novels because they 'wanted to decolonise [their] mind', and another respondent explained, 'I first read an Anita Heiss because I was trying to read books by non-white authors'. In addition to these reasons, the route-to-reader pathway is also discussed as serendipitous as evidenced in this response: '*Manhattan Dreaming* was a random selection off the shelf – I like trying out new authors and also Australian writers.'

Analysis of route-to-reader is useful in understanding the interpretative frame that readers bring to Heiss's literature. This next section considers how these diverse interpretative frames affect the readers' enjoyment of the novels. The survey asked respondents to qualify whether they enjoyed or did not enjoy the novels, and provide further details on why this was so. As with my analysis of Goodreads reviews, I coded route-to-reader responses in accordance with whether they employed the identifying language of chick lit, or exhibited a focus on the novels' politics or the author in analysis of the route-to-reader. This analysis revealed a number of interesting points. Firstly, the majority of respondents indicated that they *did* enjoy the novels. Twenty-seven respondents enjoyed the novels with only five respondents indicating that they did not. Further, in my analysis of survey respondents, more individuals were coded as using the language of politics and mention of the author than in the previous analysis of Goodreads reviews in their discussion of why they chose to read the novels. Overall, twenty-two respondents used the language of politics and mentioned the author in their route-to-reader responses. Similarly, far less route-to-reader responses employed the identifying language of chick lit than in the Goodreads reviews. This discrepancy draws attention to the nature of reviewing practice on online SRFs. Reviews on online SRFs are emotional and observably self-reflexive. The nature of these reviews, however, is subject to some variance when the reviewer is subject to more directed and contextualized questioning. The survey design presented the monograph abstract to respondents and foregrounded the 'political significance' of Heiss's novels. This variance does not diminish the content of these reader views, but merely indicates the ease with which Heiss's chick lit can be discussed through the frame of Aboriginal literature, rather than genre. Figure 3 depicts whether or not respondents enjoyed Heiss's chick lit.

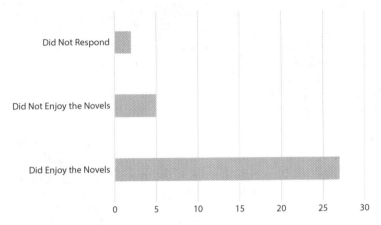

Figure 3 Whether respondents did or did not enjoy Heiss's chick lit

4.4.3 Route-to-Reader: the Language of Chick Lit

Of the seven respondents who discussed route-to-reader through the identifying language of chick lit; two indicated that they did not enjoy the novels. These two reviewers read *Not Meeting Mr Right* and *Manhattan Dreaming* and disliked the novels based on a perceived miscommunication of politics and genre. The respondent who read *Not Meeting Mr Right* wrote, 'I found the writing very transparently preachy, with little subtlety or nuance'. The novel made a significant impression on another respondent who wrote that although they 'read this book quite a while ago so my memory is not 100% fresh', there is a resounding impression of 'annoyance' with the novel: 'I do have a pretty distinct memory of being really annoyed by a lot of things like this in the novel. Every message the author wanted to convey was just really overdone or not followed up well, and to me it came off as being preachy/having certain views without having much substance behind them.' The other respondent did not enjoy *Manhattan Dreaming* based on the fact that it was marketed by their public library as 'contemporary romance' and not chick lit. They wrote, 'I was expecting a contemporary romance, not a chick-lit book.' In both cases, these novels defied these reviewers' expectations.

Overall, five respondents who used the identifying language of chick lit enjoyed the novels. Their reasons for enjoyment echo Steiner's definition of the genre (2008). One writes that *Not Meeting Mr Right*, *Avoiding Mr Right* and *Manhattan Dreaming* were 'fun easy reads with intelligent characters'. Another respondent wrote regarding the same books 'they were good fun books and I learned something about modern Aboriginal women'. Another described *Not Meeting Mr Right* as 'a light hearted and fun read with likeable characters'.

4.4.4 Route-To-Reader: the Language of Politics and the Author

Overwhelmingly more respondents – twenty-two out of thirty-four – used the language of politics and mention of the author in their discussion of route-to-reader. Although these respondents were drawn to read Heiss's chick lit because of its political dimension, few explicitly discussed this aspect of the novels in their responses. The majority of these responses – twenty out of twenty-two – indicated that they did enjoy the novels; however, most did not provide further qualification of why this was so. Seven left this section of the survey blank, a further two merely reiterated that they found Heiss's novels 'enjoyable' and another chose to discuss Heiss's memoir instead.

A small number of respondents did clearly articulate their enjoyment of the novels' political dimension. One respondent who read *Avoiding Mr Right*, *Manhattan Dreaming* and *Paris Dreaming* wrote, 'fun, light-hearted reads, dealing with more weighty topics (racism in particular) in a light-handed way'. And another who read *Paris Dreaming*, *Not Meeting Mr Right* and *Avoiding Mr Right* wrote that 'they were fun, readable character-driven stories about people, places, and relationships that were fairly familiar to me, from my own experience and/or other fiction (books/films) but with the added difference of featuring Aboriginal women, and great explorations of racial politics.' The majority of the other respondents simply discussed the novels in reference to their humour and the quality of the characterization.

Out of the thirty-four respondents, two identified as Indigenous Australian. Based on their personal identification with the novels' protagonists, both respondents enjoyed the novels: 'As an Aboriginal woman I identified with a lot of the themes.' And, 'as an Australian woman, and an Indigenous woman, it is nice to be able to find books that actually represent me. Not just the northern stereotype. The stories are fun, relevant, interesting and culturally significant.' This respondent perfectly articulates one of Heiss's authorial motivations; to write representations of Aboriginality that are under-represented.

Overall, whether respondents' route-to-reader is delineated by genre or by politics and the author, their enjoyment of the novel is not substantially affected. Readers who use the language of chick lit and readers who use the language of politics use similar language of assessment and evaluation. Heiss is, therefore, seemingly successful in reaching a diverse and broad reading audience who approach her work through different interpretative frames, but who largely draw comparable conclusions about whether they enjoyed her work. The significance of genre for Heiss's work, therefore, seems mostly in the marketing of her work. As Heiss has reflected, genre is about targeting a specific audience; however, the cogency of this frame does not seem to substantially impact the actual reading experience itself. Genre brings the reader to the page – but does not dictate the reader's experience.

4.4.5 The Cultural Interface and the Question of Education

A solid majority of survey participants responded in the affirmative when asked if they found Heiss's novels to be educational with regards to Indigenous affairs. Twenty out of thirty-four respondents found the novels to be educational, with only ten respondents suggesting that they were not.[11] It is important to note that these reviewers did not identify as Indigenous Australian.

Those that did not find the novels to be educational reached this conclusion for two primary reasons: either they did not cohere with the respondent's understanding of Aboriginality; or they felt that the novels were not written with educational intent. One respondent, who read *Avoiding Mr Right* and *Not Meeting Mr Right*, wrote:

> As I recall the books were based in an urban setting, so most of the story was very typical youngish educated female

---

[11] One respondent left this section of the survey blank.

working in the big city stuff, interwoven with life as part of
an Indigenous family. In that sense it was easy to relate to
(as at the time of reading I was of a similar demographic but
not Aboriginal).

As previously discussed, the cultural interface is the moment in which views
about Indigenous people are met with representation by Indigenous people;
that is, the moment in which Indigeneity is no longer objectified and is
instead reaffirmed by Indigenous subjectivity and experience. In this
instance, the reviewer locates Aboriginality as something distinct and outside of their own experience as an urban-based woman. This interpretation
could be reminiscent of the examples presented in Leane's (2010) work on
interpretative practices in academic classrooms, in which readers demonstrate a resistance to representations of Aboriginality outside of dominant
national stereotypes. Other respondents discussed how they did not perceive the novels to be intended to educate:

> Although I think there is some insight into the life of this
> particular Indigenous person and her family and social
> group; I have read much more interesting, engaging and
> educational books on Indigenous people and their culture –
> e.g. a range of (fiction and non-fiction) books published by
> Magabala Books. It is my view that there is a wide variety of
> Indigenous cultural perspectives and that while Heiss may
> have profile in certain markets, there are many other
> Indigenous authors who have at least as much, if not
> more, to contribute to the development of understanding
> and insight into Indigenous culture and affairs.

In a similar vein, another response established a comparison between her
chick lit novels and her memoir, thereby indicating the distinct function of
each genre:

> Not really for me – but I think I was hoping that would be
> the case. (I am sure 'Am I black enough for you?' would

teach me lots though.) That said, I think what she is doing in
this genre is valuable in that she is making ethnicity secondary to the narrative – not to devalue Indigenous culture, but
to make it less political and more accessible.

Further respondents simply identified any potential educational elements as
secondary to the plot, or completely non-apparent: 'Though there were
some references to Indigenous culture, I do not remember that aspect of the
novel being a main focus, and therefore I did not find it to be educational in
that respect.' Another wrote, 'I wasn't conscious of it.' These responses
contrast with other Goodreads reviewers' assessment of the novels as
didactic or preachy. They range from a complete lack of awareness of
these dimensions of the text, to an understanding that Heiss is producing
some innovation in genre: 'I think what she is doing in this genre is
valuable.' Overall, these responses reinforce the subjective nature of reading and the distinct expectations that readers bring to the text.

Respondents who did find the novels to be educational discussed how
the texts both furthered their awareness and provided a platform for further
engaging with Indigenous affairs. As written by one respondent:

About the best thing about this book was that it explicitly
discussed being Indigenous. As a non-Indigenous person it
definitely brought certain issues to my attention that I hadn't
encountered much before that. E.g. the idea that certain
people aren't 'black enough' to 'count' as Indigenous, that
sort of thing – and the flip side of that, potential cultural
appropriation by non-Indigenous people. However
I remember a scene where the protagonist rejects a super
white guy because he's claiming to be Indigenous – honestly
am not sure how to interpret that. But at the very least the
novel raised some awareness of these issues.

This respondent acknowledges that they gained some 'awareness' about
Aboriginality after reading *Not Meeting Mr Right*. In particular, this
included knowledge pertaining to issues around race and class. This

respondent does draw attention to the fact that the novel did not make Aboriginality totally accessible and knowable to the reader. They are left with further questions regarding issues around Aboriginal identity. Despite this, the respondent still acknowledges the importance of the novel in highlighting this issue. Similarly, another respondent who read *Manhattan Dreaming* highlights how the novel offered some new perspectives on what it was to be an urban Aboriginal woman: 'The characters were living lives similar to my own and my friends and family in many ways and it was interesting to see how their Aboriginal culture impacted on their day-to-day lives and life decisions.' This response suggests that the respondent is able to frame Aboriginality as something that is no longer distinct to the realities of urban living. In both cases, both responses highlight how these novels counter and challenge the respondent's understandings of Aboriginality.

A number of reviews indicate that they did not learn a huge amount from the novels but still reinforce their significance. One respondent who read *Paris Dreaming* and *Avoiding Mr Right* wrote, 'I didn't learn things around culture as such, but I loved how she used Indigenous culture and affairs in the plot and was able to integrate politics into the romance genre in this way.' Other respondents suggest that they already had existent knowledge about issues discussed in the novels. One respondent who read *Avoiding Mr Right* and *Not Meeting Mr Right* wrote: 'Concerns/ideas raised were already familiar as I participate as an educator in an indigenous literacy program.' Another respondent who read *Paris Dreaming* wrote: 'There were just some little bits of information that I didn't know or found interesting.' Another respondent admits to having very little knowledge prior to reading Heiss novels: 'I don't know much about Indigenous culture really and don't know anyone who is Indigenous (or at least, I don't know if they are – it's not something that's come up) so learning something new from fiction novels is always good.' This same respondent chose to read Heiss's novels *Manhattan Dreaming*, *Not Meeting Mr Right* and *Avoiding Mr Right* because they were categorized as 'romance' at their local library. This route-to-reader pathway, and the respondent's further explanation that they 'learnt something about modern Aboriginal women', demonstrates that Heiss has been successful in reaching audiences 'that weren't previously engaging with Aboriginal Australia in any format' (Heiss, 2012: 215).

To some extent, Bourdieu's demarcation of the literary field also implies distinct types of readers. Accordingly, readers of genre fiction have been theorized by Gelder (2004) as highly competent at demarcating the boundaries of the field. This understanding of the reader is formulated against a more rigid understanding of genre composed of certain formulaic elements. Reviews taken from Goodreads, and analysis of surveys conducted with respondents, however, demonstrates that the reader's understanding of genre is more porous than that expressed in scholarship. Through analysis of reader expectations, and route-to-reader, I explored the interpretative frame that readers brought to bear on Heiss's literature. Readers' interpretations of Heiss's literature was delineated by genre, by her authorial presence, and by the political dimension of the novels. Not only do these findings point to the individual and subjective nature of the reading experience in which texts are interpreted outside of their market designation, but, also, this diversity complicates academic understandings of Heiss's literature that perceive the political dimension of her novels to be in tension with the genre components of chick lit. Further, although some responses do explicitly identify Heiss's novels as educational, these responses also suggest that Heiss's literature operates as a medium for engaging readers with Aboriginal affairs with an emphasis on understanding, assistance and discussion. Instead of her literature being bluntly didactic, this approach is again more evocative of the language of reconciliation.

5 Conclusion

This Element began with a desire to explore the social significance of Heiss's chick lit. Although seemingly a simple proposition, this focus necessitated a complex and radically contextual approach that adequately accounted for the nexus of the author, text and reader. Bourdieu's conceptualization of the sociology of literature provided a powerful theoretical approach that accommodated the breadth of enquiry undertaken in this Element. His argument that meaning cannot be located within the system of texts themselves but must be understood relationally directly inspired the tripartite structure of this Element. And, although Bourdieu does not feature as centrally in this Element past Section 1, his emphasis on the social significance of literature and aversion to totalizing theoretical claims informs all subsequent sections.

Cumulatively, this Element presents a number of important findings. First and foremost, that genre remains a more porous and elusive category than is currently presented in chick lit scholarship. Not only does this Element demonstrate the limitations of scholarship based on a formulaic understanding of genre, but it also presents a less prescriptive understanding of the reader of chick lit. As evidenced in Section 4, although genre may bring the reader to the page, it does not dictate her experience or appraisal of Heiss's novels. Indeed, these readers overwhelmingly enjoyed the political aspects of these novels that do not necessarily adhere to a formulaic understanding of the genre. Overall, what was of greater importance was the quality of writing, characterization and storytelling than adherence to formula. From an authorial position, the cogency of genre is further brought into question in Section 1 in which the designation of Heiss's novels as chick lit is discussed as a marketing decision, rather than something implicit to their internal structure.

This Element also presents an argument for the political and social significance of Heiss's chick lit novels. Not only are these novels significant for their complex depiction of a nascent Aboriginal middle class but, as explored in Section 4, they are also successfully reaching a mainstream Australian audience who have not necessarily engaged with Indigenous affairs before. These findings contribute to the growing body of scholarship that explores the transformative power of literature as a medium of reconciliation.

The contextual approach presented in this Element offers potential new directions for future research on chick lit by women of colour. An intersectional ideological reading of the novels, complemented by reader response, circumvents some of the limitations of existent scholarship that focus on the irreconcilability of race and politics with the conventions of the genre. As argued by Butler and Desai in 2008, still more research is to be developed in this area.

This Element has explored Heiss's own understanding and strategizing of writing into the genre of chick lit, as well as the diverse and differentiated reader expectations that have been brought to bear on her literature. Ultimately, the analysis undertaken throughout this Element confounds academic understandings of the cogency of genre as an interpretative tool and presents new possibilities for future scholarship on chick lit.

References

Anderson, K. (2016). Bourdieu's distinction between rules and strategies and secondary principal practice: a review of selected literature. *Educational Management Administration & Leadership*, 44(4), 688–705.

Anita's Career. www.anitaheiss.com/anita_s_career. Accessed 1 June 2017.

Austlit (n.d.) A primary resource for teachers and students of Australian literature, theatre, film, television, and Aboriginal and Torres Strait Islander studies. www.austlit.edu.au.ezp.lib.unimelb.edu.au/austlit/page/A7669?mainTabTemplate=agentWorksBy&restrictToAgent=A7669&from=0&count=10000. Accessed 20 June 2018.

Ball, T. (2016). Who's afraid of the black middle class?: The socio-economic status of Aboriginals is shifting. *Meanjin*, 75(3), 81–6.

Becerra-Gurley, N. (2007). Not meeting Mr. Right. *Antipodes*, 21(2), 187–8.

Benstock, S. (2006). 'Afterword', in S. Ferriss and Y. Mallory, eds., *The New Woman's Fiction*. New York: Routledge, pp. 253–6.

Berberich, C. (ed.) (2015). *Bloomsbury Introduction to Popular Fiction*. London: Wiley Online Library.

Berlant, L. G. (1997). *The Queen of America Goes to Washington City: Essays on Sex and Citizenship*. Durham, NC: Duke University Press.

(2011). *Cruel Optimism*. Durham, NC: Duke University Press.

Berlant, L. G. and Prosser, J. (2011). Life writing and intimate publics: a conversation with Lauren Berlant. *Biography*, 34(1), 180–7.

Bharti, Santosh. (2019). The new woman in Advaita Kala's almost single. *IJELLH* (*International Journal of English Language, Literature in Humanities*), 7 (4), 872–8.

Bolt, A. (2009a). White is the new black, *Herald Sun*, 15 April.

(2009b). It's so hip to be black, *Herald Sun*, 15 April.

(2009c). White fellas in the black, *Herald Sun*, 21 August.

Bolt breached Discrimination Act, judge rules. (29 September 2011). Web. www.abc.net.au/news/2011-09-28/bolt-found-guilty-of-breaching-discrimination-act/3025918. Accessed 1 September 2018.

Bongie, C. (2008). _Friends and Enemies: the Scribal Politics of Post/Colonial Literature_. Liverpool: Liverpool University Press.

Boschetti, A. (2006). Bourdieu's work on literature: contexts, stakes and perspectives. _Theory, Culture & Society_, 23(6), 135–55.

Bourdieu, P. (1977). _Outline of a Theory of Practice_. Cambridge, UK: Cambridge University Press.

(1984). _Distinction: a Social Critique of Taste_. Translated by Richard Nice. Cambridge, MA: Harvard University Press.

(1985). The market of symbolic goods. _Poetics_, 14(1–2), 13–44.

(1988). _Homo Academicus_. Redwood, CA: Stanford University Press.

(1989). Social space and symbolic power. _Sociological theory_, 7(1), 14–25.

(1990). _The Logic of Practice_. Translated by Richard Nice. Cambridge, UK: Polity Press.

(1993). _The Field of Cultural Production_. New York: Columbia University Press.

(1996). _The Rules of Art_. Cambridge, UK: Polity Press.

(1998). _On Television_. Translated by Priscilla Parkhurst Ferguson. London: New Press.

Brewster, A. (1996). _Reading Aboriginal Women's Autobiography_. Sydney University Press.

(2007). Brokering cross-racial feminism: reading Indigenous Australian Poet Lisa Bellear. _Feminist Theory_, 8(2), 209–21.

(2008). Engaging the public intimacy of whiteness: the Indigenous protest poetry of Romaine Moreton. _Journal of the Association for the Study of Australian Literature_, Special Issue, The Colonial Present, 56–76.

(2015). *Giving this Country a Memory: Contemporary Aboriginal Voices of Australia*. New South Wales: Cambria Press.

(2016). *Reading Aboriginal Women's Life Stories*. New South Wales: Sydney University Press.

Brouillette, S. (2016). Postcolonial authorship revisited (from postcolonial writers in the global literary marketplace). In R. Dalleo, ed., *Bourdieu and Postcolonial Studies*. Liverpool: Liverpool University Press, pp. 80–97.

Brunt, K. (2007). Anita delves right into modern dating scene. *Northern Territory News*, 24 June.

Butler, K. J. (2013). *Witnessing Australian Stories: History, Testimony, and Memory in Contemporary Culture*. New York: Routledge.

Butler, P. and Desai, J. (2008). Manolos, marriage, and mantras: chick-lit criticism and transnational feminism. *Meridians*, 8(2), 1–31.

Casanova, P. (2004). *The World Republic of Letters*. Cambridge, MA: Harvard University Press.

Charmaz, K. and Bryant, A. 2008. Grounded theory. In *The SAGE Encyclopedia of Qualitative Research Methods*. Thousand Oaks: SAGE Publications, Inc, pp. 375–6. https://doi.org/10.4135/9781412963909

Chen, E. Y. (2010). Neoliberal self-governance and popular postfeminism in contemporary Anglo-American chick lit. *Concentric: Literary and cultural studies*, 36, 243–75.

Dalleo, R., ed. (2016). *Bourdieu and Postcolonial Studies*. Liverpool: Liverpool University Press.

Driscoll, B. (2014). *The New Literary Middlebrow: Tastemakers and Reading in the Twenty-First Century*. New York: Springer.

(2016). Readers of popular fiction and emotion online. In K. Gelder, ed., *New Directions in Popular Fiction*. London: Palgrave Macmillan, pp.. 425–49.

Farr, C. K. (2009). It was chick lit all along: the gendering of a genre. In L. Goren, ed., *You've Come a Long Way, Baby: Women, Politics, and Popular Culture*. University Press of Kentucky, pp. 201–14.

Fasselt, R. (2019). Crossing genre boundaries: HJ Golakai's Afropolitan chick-lit mysteries. *Feminist Theory*, 20(2), 185–200.

Ferriss, S. and Young, M. (2006). Chicks, girls and choice: redefining feminism. *Junctures: The Journal for Thematic Dialogue*, 6, 87–97.

(2006). *Chick Lit: the New Woman's Fiction*. New York: Routledge.

Fforde, C., Bamblett, L., Lovett, R., Gorringe, S. and Fogarty, B. (2013). Discourse, deficit and identity: Aboriginality, the race paradigm and the language of representation in contemporary Australia. *Media International Australia*, 149, 162–73.

Fielding, H. (1996). *Bridget Jones's Dairy*. London: Picador.

Fish, S. E. (1980). *Is There a Text in this Class?: the Authority of Interpretive Communities*. Cambridge, MA: Harvard University Press.

Foasberg, N. M. (2012). Online reading communities: from book clubs to book blogs. *The Journal of Social Media in Society*, 1(1), 30–53.

Fowler, B. (1991). *The Alienated Reader: Women and Romantic Literature in the Twentieth Century*. Hemel Hempstead: Harvester Wheatsheaf.

Frow, J. (2006). *Genre*. London: Routledge.

Fuller, D. and Rehberg Sedo, D. (2013). *Reading Beyond the Book: The Social Practices of Contemporary Literary Culture*. New York: Routledge.

Fullerton, A. (2010). From Big Merino to Big Apple. *Sun-Herald*, 8 August.

Gehrmann, S. (2019). Emerging Afro-Parisian 'chick-lit' by Lauren Ekué and Léonora Miano. *Feminist Theory*, 20(2), 215–28.

Gelder, K. (2004). *Popular Fiction: the Logics and Practices of a Literary Field*. Oxon: Routledge.

Genette, G. and Maclean, M. (1991). Introduction to the paratext. *New Literary History*, 22(2), 261–72.

Gill, R. and Herdieckerhoff, E. (2006). Rewriting the romance: new femininities in chick lit? *Feminist Media Studies*, 6(4), 487–504.

Gill, R. and Scharff, C. (eds.) (2013). *New Femininities: Postfeminism, Neoliberalism and Subjectivity*. New York: Springer.

Goodreads.com. Accessed 1 June 2016. www.goodreads.com.

Guerrero, L. A. (2006). 'Sistahs are doin' it for themselves': chick lit in black and white. In S. Ferriss and M. Young, eds., *Chick Lit: the New Women's Fiction*. New York: Routledge, pp. 87–101.

Guivarra, N. (2007). Lit Chick's Foray into 'Chick Lit'. *Koori Mail*, 28 February.

Harzewski, S. (2006). Tradition and displacement in the new novel of manners. In S. Ferriss and M. Young, eds., *Chick Lit: the New Woman's Fiction*. New York: Routledge, pp. 29–46.

(2011). *Chick Lit and Postfeminism*. Charlottesville: University of Virginia Press.

Heiss, Anita. 'anita heiss.' www.anitaheiss.com. Accessed 6 September 2018.

(1998). *Token koori*. Sydney: Curringa Communications.

(2001). *Who am I? The Diary of Mary Talence. Sydney, 1937*. NSW: Scholastic.

(2003). *Dhuuluu-Yala: To Talk Straight – Publishing Indigenous Literature*. Canberra: Aboriginal Studies Press.

(2007). *Not Meeting Mr Right*. NSW: Random House Australia.

(2008). *Avoiding Mr Right*. NSW: Random House Australia.

(2010). *Manhattan Dreaming*. NSW: Random House Australia.

(2011). *Paris Dreaming*. NSW: Random House Australia.

(2012). *Am I Black Enough For You?* NSW: Random House Australia.

(2014). Blackwords: writers on identity. *Journal of the Association for the Study of Australian Literature*, 14(3): 1–13.

(2014). *Tiddas*. New York: Simon & Schuster.

(2016). *Barbed Wire and Cherry Blossoms*. New York: Simon & Schuster.

(2017). Interview by author, 13 June.

Heiss, A. and Eastwood, D. (1996). *Sacred Cows*. Broome: Magabala Books.

Heiss, A. and Minter, P. (2014). *Macquarie Pen Anthology of Aboriginal Literature*. NSW: Allen & Unwin.

Hockx, M. and Smits, I. (2003). Theory as practice: modern Chinese literature and Bourdieu. *Reading East Asian Writing: The Limits of Literary Theory*, 12, 220–39.

hooks, b. (2000). *Where We Stand: Class Matters*. New York: Routledge.

Huggan, G. (2001). *The Postcolonial Exotic: Marketing the Margins*. New York: Routledge.

Human Rights and Equal Opportunity Commission (1997). *Bringing Them Home: National Inquiry into the Separation of Aboriginal and Torres Strait Islander Children from Their Families*. Sydney: Human Rights & Equal Opportunity Commission.

Hurt, E. (2009). Trading cultural baggage for Gucci luggage: the ambivalent Latinidad of Alisa Valdes-Rodriguez's the Dirty Girls Social Club. *MELUS: Multi-Ethnic Literature of the US*, 34(3), 133–53.

Hurt, E. (2017). Cultural citizenship and agency in the genre of chica lit and Sofia Quintero's feminist intervention. *MELUS: Multi-Ethnic Literature of the US*, 42(1), 7-31.

(2018a). *Theorizing Ethnicity and Nationality in the Chick Lit Genre*. New York: Routledge.

(2018b). The white Terry McMillan: centering black women within chick lit's genealogy. In E. Hurt, ed., *Theorizing Ethnicity and Nationality in the Chick Lit Genre*. New York: Routledge, pp.150–74.

Iser, W. (1978). *The Act of Reading: a Theory of Aesthetic Response*. Baltimore: John Hopkins University Press.

Jaivin, L. (2007). All about Anita. *Herald Sun*, 2 November.

Jauss, H. R and Benzinger, E. (1970). Literary history as a challenge to literary theory. *New Literary History*, 2(1), 7–37.

Jenkins, R. (1992). *Pierre Bourdieu: Key Sociologists*. New York: Routledge.

Johnson, R. (1993). Editor's Introduction: Pierre Bourdieu on art, literature and culture. In P. Bourdieu. *The Field of Cultural Production*. New York: Columbia University Press, pp. 1–25.

Kaye, L. (2011). Love, Paris and a few moral points. *The Age*, 4 February.

Keenan, C. (2008). The Koori Carrie. *Sun Herald*, 8 October.

Lahire, B. (2010). The double life of writers. *New Literary History*, 41(2), 439–41.

Lamaison, P. (1986). From rules to strategies: an interview with Pierre Bourdieu. *Cultural Anthropology*, 1(1), 110–20.

Langton, M. (1993). *Well, I Heard it on the Radio and I saw it on the Television ... : an Essay for the Australian Film Commission on the Politics and Aesthetics of Filmmaking by and about Aboriginal People and Things*. Sydney: Australian Film Commission Sydney.

(2012). Counting our victories: the end of Garvey-Ism and the soft bigotry of low expectation. *Boyer Lecture Series*. 16 December. *www.abc.net.au/radionational/programs/boyerlectures/series/2012-boyer-lectures/4305696*. Accessed 26 November 2020.

Leane, J. (2010). Aboriginal representation: conflict or dialogue in the academy. *The Australian Journal of Indigenous* Education, 39(1), 32–9.

(2014). Tracking our country in settler literature. *Journal of the Association for the Study of Australian Literature*, 14(3), 1–17.

(2016). Other peoples' stories: when is writing cultural appropriation? *Overland*, 225, 41.

Long, E. (2003). *Book Clubs: Women and the Uses of Reading in Everyday Life*. Chicago: University of Chicago Press.

Ludlow, F., Baker, L., Brock, S., Hebdon, C. and Dove, M. (2016). The double binds of indigeneity and indigenous resistance. *Humanities*, 5(3), 53.

Mabry, A. R. (2006). About a girl: female subjectivity and sexuality in contemporary 'chick'. In S. Ferriss and M. Young, eds., *Chick Lit: the New Woman's Fiction*. New York: Routledge, pp. 191–206.

Malik, A. (2019). Chick lit as a trajectory of Jean Baudrillard's the consumer society: an Indian perspective. *IJELLH (International Journal of English Language, Literature in Humanities)*, 7,13–13.

Mathew, I. (2016a). The pretty and the political didn't seem to blend well': Anita Heiss's chick lit and the destabilisation of a genre. *Journal of the Association for the Study of Australian Literature*, 15(3), 1–11.

(2016b). Educating the reader in Anita Heiss's chick lit. *Contemporary Women's Writing*, 10(3), 334–53.

(2016c). Reviewing race in the digital literary sphere: a case study of Anita Heiss' am I black enough for you? *Australian Humanities Review*, 60, 65–83.

Merrick, E. (2006). *This Is Not Chick Lit: Original Stories by America's Best Women Writers (No Heels Required)*. New York: Random House.

Meyer, Neele. (2018). Challenging gender and genre: women in contemporary Indian crime fiction in English. *Zeitschrift für Anglistik und Amerikanistik*. 66, 105–17.

Mißler, H. (2016). *The Cultural Politics of Chick Lit: Popular Fiction, Postfeminism and Representation*. New York: Routledge.

Moi, T. (1997). The challenge of the particular case: Bourdieu's sociology of culture and literary criticism. *Modern Language Quarterly*, 58(4), 497.

Moji, P. B. (2018). Divas and deviance: hip-hop feminism and black visuality in Lauren Ekué's Icône Urbaine (2006). *Agenda*. 32(3), 10–20.

Montoro, R. (2012). *Chick Lit: The Stylistics of Cappuccino Fiction*. New York: Bloomsbury Publishing.

Moreton-Robinson, A. (2000). *Talkin'up to the White Woman: Aboriginal Women and Feminism*. Queensland: University of Queensland Press.

Morrison, A. M. 2010. Chicanas and 'chick lit': contested Latinidad in the novels of Alisa Valdes-Rodriguez. *The Journal of Popular Culture*, 43(2), 309–29.

Muecke, S. (1992). *Textual Spaces: Aboriginality and Cultural Studies*, Sydney: New South Wales University Press.

Naik, Y. (2012). Finding good reads on Goodreads: readers take RA into their own hands. *Reference & User Services Quarterly*, 51(4), 319.

Nakamura, L. (2013). 'Words with friends': socially networked reading on Goodreads. *PMLA*, 128(1), 238–43.

Nakata, M. N. (2007). *Disciplining the Savages, Savaging the Disciplines*. Canberra: Aboriginal Studies Press.

Newns, L. (2018). Renegotiating romantic genres: textual resistance and Muslim chick lit. *The Journal of Commonwealth Literature*, 53(2), 284–300.

Ogunnaike, L. (2004). Black writers seize glamorous ground around 'Chick Lit'. *New York Times*, 31 May.

O'Mahony, L. (2018). More than sex, shopping, and shoes: cosmopolitan indigeneity and cultural politics in Anita Heiss's Koori lit. In E. Hurt, ed., *Theorizing Ethnicity and Nationality in the Chick Lit Genre*. New York/London: Routledge, pp. 41–68.

Ommundsen, W. (2011). Sex and the global city: chick lit with a difference. *Contemporary Women's Writing*, 5(2), 107–24.

O'Reilly, N. (ed.) (2010). *Postcolonial Issues in Australian Literature*. New York: Cambria Press.

Our Koorie Carrie busy avoiding Mr Right. (2008). *Geelong Advertiser*, 8 September.

Pearson, N. (2016). Soft bigotry holds back Indigenous reform. *The Australian*, 10 December.

Pham, K. (2017, 1 July). Indigenous author Anita Heiss opens new chapter at UC. www.canberra.edu.au. Accessed 2 June 2018.

Radway, J. (1984). *Reading the Romance: Women, Patriarchy, and Popular Culture*, London: The University of North Carolina Press.

Ramírez, C. S. (2009). End of Chicanismo: Alisa Valdes-Rodriguez's Dirty Girls. https://rca.ucsc.edu/documents/report-02-ramirez.pdf. Accessed 2 June 2018.

Reconciliation Australia. Strategic Plan 2017–2022. www.reconciliation .org.au/wp-content/uploads/2017/12/ra-strategic-plan_web.pdf. Accessed 16 December 2017.

Rehberg Sedo, D. (2003). Readers in reading groups: an online survey of face-to-face and virtual book clubs. *Convergence*, 9(1), 67–90.

   (2011) *Reading Communities From Salons to Cyberspace.* New York: Springer.

   (2017). Reading reception in the digital era. *Oxford Research Encyclopedias.* http://literature.oxfordre.com/view/10.1093/acrefore/9780190201098 .001.0001/acrefore-9780190201098-e-285. Accessed 6 September 2018.

Rowntree, M., Moulding, N. and Bryant, L. (2012). Feminine sexualities in chick lit. *Australian Feminist Studies*, 27(72), 121–37.

Scott, R. and Heiss, A. (eds.) (2015). *The Intervention: an Anthology.* Australia: Griffin Press.

Séllei, N. (2006). Bridget Jones and Hungarian chick lit. In S. Ferriss and M. Young, eds., *Chick Lit: the New Woman's Fiction.* New York: Routledge, pp. 173–88.

Speller, J. R. W. (2013). *Bourdieu and Literature.* Cambridge, UK: Open Book Publishers.

Spencer, L. G. (2019). 'In defence of chick-lit': refashioning feminine subjectivities in Ugandan and South African contemporary women's writing. *Feminist Theory*, 20(2), 155–69.

Steiner, A. (2008). Private criticism in the public space: personal writing on literature in readers' reviews on Amazon. *Participations*, 5(2) www.participations.org/Volume%205/Issue%202/5_02_steiner.htm. Accessed 25 January 2017.

Swann, J. and Allington, D. (2009). Reading groups and the language of literary texts: a case study in social reading. *Language and Literature*, 18(3), 247–64.

Thelwall, M. and Kousha, K. (2017). Goodreads: a social network site for book readers. *Journal of the Association for Information Science and Technology*, 68(4), 972–83.

Tuchman, G. and Fortin, N. E. (1989). *Edging Women Out: Victorian Novelists, Publishers and Social Change*. Oxon: Routledge.

Umminger, A. (2006). Supersizing Bridget Jones: what's really eating the women in chick lit. In S. Ferriss and M. Young, eds., *Chick Lit: The New Woman's Fiction*. New York: Routledge, pp. 239–52.

Valenzuela, A. (2018). Chica lit: popular Latina fiction and Americanization in the twenty-first century by Tace Hedrick. *Studies in Latin American Popular Culture*, 36, 180–2.

Verboord, M. (2014). The impact of peer-produced criticism on cultural evaluation: a multilevel analysis of discourse employment in online and offline film reviews. *New Media & Society*, 16(6), 921–40.

Vlieghe, J., Muls, J. and Rutten, K. 2016. Everybody reads: reader engagement with literature in social media environments. *Poetics*, 54, 25–37.

Wolfe, P. (2006). Settler colonialism and the elimination of the native. *Journal of Genocide Research*, 8(4), 387–409.

Yardley, C. (2006). *Will Write for Shoes: How to Write a Chick Lit Novel*. New York: Thomas Dunne Books.

Cambridge Elements ≡

Publishing and Book Culture

SERIES EDITOR

Samantha Rayner
University College London

Samantha Rayner is a Reader in UCL's Department of Information Studies. She is also Director of UCL's Centre for Publishing, co-Director of the Bloomsbury CHAPTER (Communication History, Authorship, Publishing, Textual Editing and Reading) and co-editor of the Academic Book of the Future BOOC (Book as Open Online Content) with UCL Press.

ASSOCIATE EDITOR

Leah Tether
University of Bristol

Leah Tether is Professor of Medieval Literature and Publishing at the University of Bristol. With an academic background in medieval French and English literature and a professional background in trade publishing, Leah has combined her expertise and developed an international research profile in book and publishing history from manuscript to digital.

ABOUT THE SERIES

This series aims to fill the demand for easily accessible, quality texts available for teaching and research in the diverse and dynamic fields of Publishing and Book Culture. Rigorously researched and peer-reviewed Elements will be published under themes, or 'Gatherings'. These Elements should be the first check point for researchers or students working on that area of publishing and book trade history and practice: we hope that, situated so logically at Cambridge University Press, where academic publishing in the UK began, it will develop to create an unrivalled space where these histories and practices can be investigated and preserved.

Cambridge Elements ≡

Publishing and Book Culture
Women, Publishing, and Book Culture

Gathering Editor: Rebecca Lyons
Rebecca Lyons is a Teaching Fellow at the University of
Bristol. She is also co-editor of the experimental BOOC (Book
as Open Online Content) at UCL Press. She teaches and
researches book and reading history, particularly female
owners and readers of Arthurian literature in fifteenth- and
sixteenth-century England, and also has research interests in
digital academic publishing.

ELEMENTS IN THE GATHERING

Aboriginal Writers and Popular Fiction: The Literature of Anita Heiss
Fiannuala Morgan

A full series listing is available at: www.cambridge.org/EPBC

Printed in the United States
By Bookmasters